Seven Secrets
Cookbook

Healthy Cuisine
Your Family Will Love

Seven Secrets Cookbook offers recipes using only plant foods
or unrefined plant products that not only are delicious
but will help you stay well and trim.

Neva & Jim Brackett

REVIEW AND HERALD® PUBLISHING ASSOCIATION
HAGERSTOWN, MD 21740

The Review and Herald® Publishing Association publishes biblically based materials for spiritual, physical, and mental growth and Christian discipleship.

The authors assume full responsibility for the accuracy of all facts and quotations as cited in this book.

Texts credited to NIV are from the *Holy Bible, New International Version.* Copyright © 1973, 1978, 1984, International Bible Society. Used by permission of Zondervan Bible Publishers.

Texts credited to NKJV are from the New King James Version. Copyright © 1979, 1980, 1982 by Thomas Nelson, Inc. Used by permission. All rights reserved.

This book was
Edited by Kathy Page and Shirley Mulkern
Copyedited by James Cavil
Food design by Kimberly Fisher
Interior design and photograpy by Jim Brackett
Cover design by Patricia Wegh
Cover photo by Joel D. Springer

Printed in U.S.A.

R&H Cataloging Service
Brackett, Neva and Jim
    Seven secrets cookbook: cuisine your family will love, by Neva and Jim Brackett.
    1. Vegetarian cooking.   I. Brackett, Neva.   II. Title

ISBN 10: 0-8280-1995-9
ISBN 13: 978-0-8280-1995-8

Neva and Jim Brackett have also written *Best Gourmet Recipes* and *Something Better* (now out of print). *Seven Secrets Cookbook* contains more than 200 recipes or variations, only a few of which appeared in these earlier cookbooks.

To order *Seven Secrets Cookbook or Best Gourmet Recipes,* **call 1-800-765-6955.**
Visit us at **www.reviewandherald.com** for information on these and other Review and Herald® products.

CONTENTS

Ice Cream on Waffles, p. 16

Vegetarian Cheese Pizza, p. 30

Fruit Pizza, p. 86

Neva Brackett knew little about cooking when she was first married, but put her mind to every opportunity and, under the blessing of God, has become a premiere vegetarian cook. We tell this part of the story so that everyone will be encouraged to know they can do it too! She has learned how to make healthy food taste good and passes along the secrets to those who wish to learn. After all, if healthy food tasted good, your family would probably have no problem following a better plan!

She and her husband, Jim, have held nutrition seminars and cooking classes for nearly 30 years in hundreds of locations across America and in other countries. Neva was also the food service manager at Five Loaves Deli and Bakery for 10 years, where in some cases customers traveled two hours and more just to have breakfast at the Sunday brunch.

Their greatest reward for the year of almost non-stop work to complete this book will be an improvement in your health! We trust it can be a whole-person endeavor, physically, mentally and spiritually.

SEVEN SECRETS, as with Neva Brackett's earlier books, has been a family effort. For nearly 10 years, when high school and college was not in session, Kathy and Kim worked at Five Loaves Deli and Bakery, the vegetarian restaurant in Seattle that Jim and Neva had opened. The girls became excellent chefs in their own right, and many of the recipes in SEVEN SECRETS are theirs. Kim has done most of the food design, and Jim did the photography, design, and layout. Kathy, with a natural gift to write, prepared much of the script.

We wrote *Seven Secrets* because we want to help you improve your family's health. The fact that you are holding this book indicates that you are interested in cooking healthy meals. But maybe you aren't sure how to do it. We frequently read or hear in the media advice from leading nutritionists, scientists, and physicians on what we should be eating. But it isn't easy to make lifestyle changes, especially when it comes to changing what we eat.

> *If healthful food tasted good, you and your family would be happy to eat it!*

Eating delicious food is a delightful experience. But we Westerners have developed a taste for food that is risky to our health. And we have lost the skills (and determination) needed to prepare healthful food that is also tasty and attractive. *Seven Secrets* can help change that. We know that if healthful food tasted good, looked appealing, and was affordable, you and your family would be happy to eat it!

Let me share a little about how we came to write a cookbook. For 10 years we owned and managed two vegetarian restaurants in Seattle: Five Loaves Deli and Bakery and The Pocket Place. Neva and her staff served thousands of meals using healthy recipes similar to the ones you'll find in this book. And for 30 years we've conducted hundreds of cooking classes all over the United States—even some in other countries.

How can you get your family to adopt more healthy eating habits? It will take some willingness to allow their tastes to change gradually. At our restaurants almost everyone enjoyed these healthy dishes. Every recipe may not be a winner for everyone, but here are some suggestions that we believe will help you introduce healthy food to your family.

1. Go slowly. Don't clear the meat, dairy, and oil out of your kitchen all at once. Add one new meal to your menu at a time. Soon it will become a family favorite.

2. Serve your first dish without fanfare. Don't announce, "This is healthy!" or "This is cashew cheese!" Cashews can never be cheese. But that entrée will be delicious because of the nuts, and they won't miss the cheese if you don't mention it.

3. Heart disease or diabetes can be dramatically reversed for many people. If you or someone in your family has one of those conditions, you'll want to make changes more rapidly. Go ahead! Get rid of the culprit foods and make a new shopping list based on this book. Just be sure you make changes deliberately and steadily.

You will notice that there is a spiritual flavor in *Seven Secrets*. This is because we believe that our bodies belong to God—a concept found in the Bible. We believe that the best health will result when you accept your God-given responsibility to keep your body as healthy as possible. (You'll

> *The best health will result when you accept your God-given responsibility to keep your body as healthy as possible.*

enjoy reading Neva's story on page 116, where she recounts how unskilled she was in the kitchen until God answered her prayer for help.) No matter what your spiritual values are, we're sure you will benefit from making healthy food taste good.

In the recipe sections of *Seven Secrets* there are frequent references to other recipes in the book. In order to help you find them quickly, we have indicated these in red type. Ingredients that may be less familiar to the average cook appear in blue type and are discussed in Shopping Secrets and Glossary. This section also tells you where to buy lesser-known products.

> *In the back of the book we have included Efficiency Tips, the result of many years of experience in saving time.*

People are often concerned that if they quit using so many refined or prepared products, it will take more time in the kitchen—efficiency can make up for much of it! So in the back of the book we have included Efficiency Tips, the result of many years of experience in saving time.

The Ingredient Equivalents section gives general guidelines for substitutions—a real plus if something is missing from your pantry. Another helpful section in the back of the book is Menus and Shopping Lists. This section provides complete menus with shopping lists—enough for four weeks! This will help you get a running start on what to plan for the family and what to keep on your pantry shelf.

If you have children or grandchildren, you'll appreciate Favorites for Children. These are recipes kids especially enjoy eating. You may even get them into the kitchen to help you make the healthy and delicious dishes!

There are two indexes in the very back of the book. The Topical Index lists recipes by type and indicates which are wheat-free. The Recipe Index lists all the recipes alphabetically; if a recipe has two or more words, you will find it listed under each of the prominent words in the title. So "Carob Dessert Trifle" would also be listed as "Trifle, Carob Dessert" and "Dessert Trifle, Carob."

Finally, we make every effort to use only unrefined plant products. There are some exceptions mainly in the use of sweeteners and also in an effort to "reach out" to family members who may not be ready to follow the very best dietary plan for their health or at least not without the changes taking more time. We often use dates, raisins, or some other whole food sweetener, but also use some honey, syrup, or sugar of some kind, though sparingly. It is certainly possible for one to use some refined flour, for example, in a recipe, in an effort to make a preparation a little more like the standard fare.

Lower Your Cholesterol Without Medication!
Prevent or Even Reverse Diabetes!
Drastically Lower Your Risk of Heart Disease!

Are these preposterous claims? No, these claims are substantiated in medical literature—here is how you can do it. Let's begin with the issue of controlling our weight.

Most Americans are overweight. In the past two decades this condition has increased to pandemic proportions: 60 to 80 percent of adults are overweight. Many are in the obese category.[1] These extra pounds are making us more susceptible to a host of health problems from heart disease to diabetes to certain cancers, and much more.

If you're tired of being too heavy, take a look at this unique non-diet plan!

Very few of us are pleased with the extra pounds we are carrying, although some of us have developed a jolly spirit in an attempt to relieve our private agony. Recently I worked with a woman who weighed nearly 500 pounds. As time went by she confided to me her innermost feelings: "When I go to an all-you-can-eat restaurant, people look at me and think, *What are you doing in here, you big fat slob?*" Those were her tragic words, not mine. Her negativity is a common thread among overweight people.

Solutions, of course, are offered everywhere. Friends offer unsolicited advice and advertisers promise pills to suppress hunger and burn calories. These slick and convincing ads seldom reveal the research: less than 5 percent of Americans who diet keep the weight off long-term. Most of us know that from painful experience.

"But," you ask, "how do I know your plan is not just another empty promise?" That's a fair question. You will need a certain degree of trust to accept our proposed eating plan, but it might help you to know that we have nothing to sell. It will cost you less than what you are doing now. The approach is very simple: You essentially eat all you want and lose weight slowly and consistently—and keep it off as long as you stay with the plan.

"Wait a minute," you say. "All the plans work if you stay with them!" True. Most dieters gain their weight back because they quit the diet. But there are three great differences with this plan.

1. You eat all you want.[2]

2. No spending money on a "weight loss" product.

3. You don't diet, you *live it*. This is a new lifestyle—one so workable and energizing that you will never want the old one back. So what is this plan? Here it is in one simple sentence: Exercise moderately and eat only unrefined plant foods.

You're probably wondering, *Is that a life? Where will I get the energy to exercise? How can I turn down favorite foods while people all around me, some of them thin, enjoy the American diet?* One key is to visualize success. See yourself buying new clothes, several sizes smaller. Imagine a life of looking and feeling great. That is a life!

Exercise

Every diet requires exercise to be effective. It not only burns calories, but raises the efficiency of your gigantic calorie burner, the basal metabolic rate (BMR). Every day the body needs a certain amount of calories just to operate, even if we don't move a muscle all day. The basal metabolic rate is the calories burned to pump blood, breathe, run the brain, process food, keep the body warm, etc. The astonishing thing is that this BMR for most people is about 75 percent of their total calorie expenditure—close to 1,500 calories. You'd need to run 15 miles to burn 1,500 calories! Many people burn only an additional 300 calories for a whole day's activities (the equivalent of walking three miles).

Here's the catch: If you diet, your BMR, which is the giant calorie consumer, will decrease. It is as though the body says to itself, "Food shortage! Conserve calories!" The body turns down the "furnace." Exercise tricks the body into keeping the furnace going full-blast even on fewer calories. The food shortage is ignored when you exercise, and your body burns calories left and right.

Most people will need to walk three miles per day to make this work.[3] Any form of exercise will do. Try to find something you enjoy: play tennis, ride a bike, go swimming, or work in your garden. Just find out how long it takes you to walk three miles, and then exercise that long each day. And you don't have to ex-

---

This young woman lost 90 pounds in one year!

---

ercise vigorously. You can even divide up your three miles throughout the day and you will burn the same number of calories. You can even exercise leisurely. Whether you run or walk that mile, slow or fast, the same number of calories will be burned.

What's more, for about a day after exercise (and if the exercise is vigorous, the effect is greater) the BMR is even higher, giving you added help in controlling calories. Amazingly, a sedentary person (very little exercise) will tend to have a larger appetite than one who has been exercising regularly.[4]

The *Live It*

Start with delicious produce, grains, and nuts. Thoughtfully prepare them in your own kitchen. Then sit down and enjoy several helpings, guilt-free. Unrefined plant foods are naturally low in fat. That helps you to lose weight, because a low-fat meal has fewer calories but still fills you up. A pound of fat has more than twice the calories of a pound of carbohydrate or protein. A meal from this cookbook might have half the calories of the meal you ate last night!

What *did* you eat last night? If you had a serving or two of vegetables and salad, good for you! But you may be struggling with extra weight because you're eating refined foods: dressings, gravies, sauces, and entrées. The term *refined foods* refers to the process of removing fiber and nutrients from plant foods, and usually increasing the amount of fat. There is another way to eat your entrées, potatoes, fruit, and vegetables! You don't have to eat them plain—you'll learn about that in the recipes that follow.

Refined foods can be blamed for most of the excess pounds people carry around. The culprits are oil, butter, and the high percentage of fat found in meat. Neva replaces oil in her recipes with nuts, olives, and coconut. Those foods give you all the moisture you need and make the food taste great, but because the refining process is left behind, you don't get too many calories.

Obviously junk food is highly refined. A 200-calorie potato becomes a 1,000-calorie bag of chips. Chips are easy to eat, and even easier to store as fat. Other refined foods, such as white bread, pasta, and rice, are not as fattening but should be replaced with their whole-grain originals. Fewer calories are consumed, while the fiber and nutrients your body needs are restored.

Read the Label!

If the label says "wheat flour" it is refined. If it's unrefined the label will say 100 percent whole wheat (or some other grain). Often both kinds of flour will be listed, and if that's the case, don't buy it. Also, watch for added fat in various forms—lard, butter,

---

"Something better" is the watchword. Don't ask someone to give up something unless you have something better to offer them.

---

margarine, vegetable oil, or partially hydrogenated oil—don't buy it! This will eliminate perhaps 97 out of 100 loaves of bread on the shelf at the store. If you want to control your weight, all your food needs to be unrefined!

Will you get hungry two hours after eating our low-fat recipes? No! Recently I was visiting with a physician who wanted a better understanding of this concept, and she said, "But fat is needed for satiety." In other words, since fat slows digestion time it tends to keep us satisfied, keeps us from getting hungry too quickly. She was right. It is the fat that makes us feel full. But there is another ingredient usually missing from processed foods that also provides satiety: fiber. Plant foods are all high in fiber, but the fiber is removed when processed into white bread or pasta, vegetable oil, and sugar. These are just the obvious examples.

Animal products don't need to be processed or refined to lose fiber—they never had fiber, they never will! Don't miss this incredible point: Animal products (meat, fish, chicken, eggs, and milk) have *zero* fiber. No wonder so many Americans are constipated. Of course, fiber has much more to offer besides regularity. It lowers cholesterol. It helps protect against diabetes. And it helps keep us from getting hungry too quickly so we don't look for snacks.

The recipes in this cookbook are different—they don't use animal products. The ingredients are from your garden or the produce department, tastefully presented with gravies, sauces, and dressings made from nuts. All the fiber is still there. When you eat your first meal from this book, you will agree with the participants in our weight-loss programs. They were amazed to find that they could go five hours without even a snack—they just never felt hungry.

The *live it* is not just for weight control. Cholesterol goes down, the cholesterol ratio is improved, and hypertension can be cured and controlled. There is a much decreased risk for a number of cancers. There is a dramatic decrease in diabetes incidence, with a virtual nonincidence of gout.

Shannon was not only tall (6'3") but well endowed with extra pounds. We hired her as a favor to an old friend to work in Five Loaves Deli and Bakery, our vegetarian restaurant. "Watch out for the ice-cream machine!" warned her mother, who doubted she could lose weight with free ice cream around. But Shannon lost weight! And so did nearly every other employee. They ate many of their meals at the restaurant and followed this plan for meals eaten away from work. Slowly the extra pounds would come off and normal weight would stabilize. Shannon lost 90 pounds in one year! For exercise she rode her bicycle several times a week. She ate all she wanted, including the healthy ice cream we'll teach you to make, and still lost those 90 pounds.

Finally, a word about the psychology of controlling weight. Through a complex interplay of one's background and life experiences it's possible to develop a true obsession to overeating. There are people who almost tear the doors off the cupboards to get food, stuffing themselves as fast as they can gulp it down, not even enjoying the food. This is the extreme end of the spectrum, but if you recognize something like this in yourself, you need more help than this book can offer. See a physician and get help in finding professionals to guide you through recovery from a very complex problem.

—Jim Brackett, M.A., M.P.H.

---

[1]*Overweight* is defined by the World Health Organization as a body mass index of 25 or more, obesity a BMI of 30 or more, and morbid obesity a BMI over 35. Your body mass index is easy to calculate on the Web at http://nhlbisupport.com/bmi/ by simply entering your height and weight into the appropriate place—the calculation is done for you. You can calculate it yourself by following this formula: BMI = 703 x (weight in pounds)/[(height in inches)(height in inches)].

[2]If you "stuff" yourself or eat large quantities of high-calorie plant foods, you can get too many calories even with unrefined plant foods. The four plant categories that are high in fat are nuts, seeds, avocados, and olives.

[3]If you cannot walk this much because of excess weight, disability, or pain, you may want to try walking in water. As you step into a pool, the pain lessens or ceases as the water reaches the painful places. The secret is the buoyancy provided by the water—you weigh less in water so the stress on your muscles and joints is decreased. Once you find a depth that makes walking possible, stay at that depth and walk back and forth across the pool. It has been shown in studies that consistent "conductor motion" (such as moving your arms) several times each day for about 10 minutes at a time makes a demonstrable difference.

[4]Up to a point, of course. If the average exercise is more substantial, the appetite will begin to increase to care for the extra need. This crossover point is likely different for individuals but is in the realm of about three miles walking per day.

THE SEVEN SECRETS TO DELIGHTFUL FOOD

In order to make plant based foods tasteful and attractive, we have discovered seven basic areas of food preparation and some simple skills that will make all the difference. Thus the recipe section in *Seven Secrets* is the practical application of seven basic principles—simple secrets of making scrumptious meals that make you forget you're eating healthy!

1. USE WHOLE GRAINS IN PLACE OF REFINED, AND STILL ENJOY YOUR FOOD.

2. REPLACE BUTTER, OIL, AND EGGS IN BAKING WITHOUT SACRIFICING TENDERNESS AND TASTE.

3. MAKE WHITE OR CHEESE SAUCE TO USE IN PLACE OF MILK AND CHEESE, AND YET ENJOY CREAMY, DELICIOUS ENTRÉES AND SOUPS.

4. REPLACE MEAT, AND STILL BE ABLE TO ADAPT YOUR FAVORITE RECIPES WITH HEALTHFUL ALTERNATIVES.

5. FRY OR SAUTÉE WITHOUT OIL, ELIMINATING A SIGNIFICANT SOURCE OF DAMAGING FAT IN YOUR FOOD.

6. MAKE A GOOD SPREAD OR DRESSING FOR BREAD AND SALAD. AFTER ALL, IT'S WHAT WE PUT ON THE BREAD, POTATOES, OR SALAD THAT MAKES THEM FATTENING.

7. CUT DOWN ON REFINED SUGAR

As you put these basic skills into practice, you will see that these recipes are not so new and strange after all. They are just new variations of an old familiar theme. Something new and unfamiliar seems ard at first, but after the skill has been tried and learned, you realize how very simple it really is! If you will take the time to become familiar with these few basic techniques, you will have the secret to success.

The lifestyle of adequate exercise and healthier foods presented in the previous section will prevent almost everyone from getting type 2 diabetes.[1] The same plan will reduce cholesterol in the blood and lower the risk of coronary artery disease. It will help 40 percent or more of those with diabetes to recover—they can have normal blood sugar and significantly reverse some of the damage diabetes has caused. If they follow the program carefully, the average time required to get well is three to six weeks, although some people respond in days. Nearly 90 percent of peripheral neuropathy disappears, and almost everyone finds relief from this often very painful condition within a few days. (Some have complete freedom from pain in just two days.)

How do I know? I've seen it happen at Weimar Institute, which is located near Sacramento, California. Neva and I have had the privilege of working with the Weimar physicians in the Reversing Diabetes program for more than 10 years (either http://newstart.com/diabetes.html or www.reversingdiabetes.org) and have seen these results ourselves countless times.

In order to reverse diabetes, we use the same plan as for losing weight: moderate daily activity[2] and all food from unrefined plant products. (Be sure to read the previous section since we won't repeat many of the same important points here.)

In the weight-control program we encourage participants to move judiciously but steadily. For diabetics the case is more urgent. If the hemoglobin A1c (also known as glycosylated hemoglobin) is above 6.0 percent, significant damage is taking place to virtually every tissue in the body. In fact, the medical community has concluded that if there is diabetes, then there is heart disease! So in order to halt the progressive damage, a diabetic needs to make these changes now! They must follow the plan religiously if they want to get well. Certainly there will be improvement if they make some changes, but to have normal sugar without medication requires strict adherence.

Nearly 90 percent of peripheral neuropathy disappears.

These changes are challenging for most people, but they can be done with reasonable effort and determination. We have followed this exercise and healthful-food plan ourselves for more than 30 years, and our health is great! And the food is really good. In fact, if you could eat at our home or at one of the Reversing Diabetes seminars, I believe you would proclaim, "I'd be happy to eat like this all the time—it's wonderful!"

As in weight control, this plan calls for a reasonable amount of walking, two or three plant-based meals each day (the first meal is the largest and lesser ones follow), and no snacking at all.

Sometimes a physician may advise a patient to eat many smaller meals each day with less carbohydrate and more protein—almost the exact opposite of what we are proposing here. The physicians make these suggestions largely because patients usually won't do what is best. Carbohydrate is the preferred food for the trillion cells in your body. The reason a physician suggests a cutback is that Americans eat mostly refined carbohydrates.

The fad for "low-carb" regimens is highly flawed. Rather than helping us eat unrefined carbs, which is just what our body needs, it recommends that we increase fat and protein and reduce carbs. This is hard on our kidneys and produces high levels of toxins in the blood. In fact, before the most well known of the low-carb programs was recently revised, the user had to test the urine several times each day for ketones (organic byproducts from burning fat). Since the high-protein diet could cause damage and even death from ketoacidosis, the ketone level had to be carefully monitored.

Plant foods are low in fat and protein and high in carbs, except four categories that are high in fat (and therefore high in calories)—olives, avocados, nuts, and seeds. We need to eat these more sparingly. A good handful each day would be a reasonable goal. It has been shown in recent years that nuts (of all kinds) lower the incidence of heart disease.[3]

Which brings us to the second reason physicians sometimes advise many small high-protein, high-fat, low-carb meals for the diabetic. If we use refined carbohydrate without the fiber that is naturally in the plant foods, our blood sugar rises quickly to high levels following a meal. Since we either won't or don't know how to prepare our foods with unrefined carbohydrates, which would lower blood sugar, the physician throws up his or her hands and says, "Well, use a low-carb plan," even though it's not really a solution. This plan may help in a small degree to keep sugar levels from soaring, but it's truly a band-aid approach.

Don't miss this all-important point: unrefined plant foods have fiber—and in just the right proportions. Animal products have *zero* fiber—in other words, all meat (including fish, chicken, and seafood) and other animal products, such as milk, eggs, and cheese, have absolutely no fiber at all! Around the world, cultures that use animal products and refined plant products and that include too many calories and too little exercise (the standard Western lifestyle) have increasingly high levels of diabetes.

Fiber is defined as that portion of the food that is indigestible. It is found in plants in two broad categories—soluble and insoluble. The soluble fiber soaks up moisture and makes a kind of gelatinous slurry (a little bit like Jell-O) in the small intestine. This slows the movement of nutrients so that the meal is "delivered" to the bloodstream in five to six hours rather than in a much shorter time. This long-lasting, smooth delivery of nutrients (including sugar) allows the body to control blood sugar levels. If refined carbs are in our food, there are blood sugar spikes followed by dramatic lows as the body struggles to control the unexpected surges of nutrient delivery.

Imagine a group of people standing in a swimming pool filled with shoulder-deep molasses. Let's say they are instructed to get out of the pool as fast as possible. They struggle through the thick goo to the pool edge and climb out. Obviously it would take much longer to get out than if the pool had water in it. Let's let the pool represent the small intestine and the people represent the nutrients that are being ab-

sorbed into the bloodstream (leaving the pool). The fiber turns the water in the pool into molasses. A refined diet would result in a more "waterlike" environment in the small intestines! A slower delivery of nutrients to the bloodstream is critical for good health.

Another benefit from fiber, though not such an immediate issue in diabetes, is that the insoluble fiber binds itself to the bile our bodies make (almost pure cholesterol) and other forms of cholesterol that come from our diet. These "hooked-together" molecules of cholesterol and fiber are too large to be absorbed into the bloodstream and so are excreted—which means this bound cholesterol is not absorbed into the blood. The obvious effect is a lowering of our (blood serum) cholesterol.

The physicians we work with in the Reversing Diabetes program believe that approximately 65 to 70 percent of a diabetic's recovery is from exercise. They have found that diabetics aren't likely to get well unless they exercise at a level equivalent to walking four miles each day.

Let's explore a basic reason that exercise is so critical. Approximately 10 years before a person is diagnosed with diabetes the amount of insulin in the blood begins to rise. The body is doing this in order to force the increasing blood sugar levels from the blood into the cells—thus lowering or controlling blood sugar. This increase in the amount of insulin needed to "control" the blood sugar is called insulin resistance. The problem isn't exactly that the body is resisting insulin. Rather the problem is that the cells are making less and less of a substance needed to move sugar from the outside of the cell to the inside. These little sugar movers have a large name,[4] which isn't at all important to understanding the issue. The point is that the insulin receptor on the cell is activated by insulin to send a message to the DNA to make these sugar movers—and right here is the problem. The message is sent, but it receives an increasingly smaller response—over the years, less and less of the sugar movers are produced. The body's reaction is to make more insulin to send more messages, which helps in a degree but eventually fails to control the sugar level

> *Sixty-five to 70 percent of the recovery is from exercise.*

adequately. Now the body has very high levels of insulin, but the messages to make sugar movers are so poorly heeded that the sugar level in the bloodstream rises and the person becomes diabetic.

Diabetics have heard that they can take oral medication and help the situation. Although physicians have attempted to lower A1c scores to 6.0 percent with medication, the medical community has recently acknowledged that this is not achievable in most patients, so a goal of 7.0 percent is now seen as a reasonable target. Reasonable not because that's safe for the diabetic (it isn't), but because that's about the best we can do with medication.

In reality, it would be better to use insulin,[5] because that is a substance natural to the body. But the average diabetic has somehow gotten the idea that when you finally have to go on the needle, death is near. But in reality, it isn't the needle or the insulin that brings one closer to the end—it's simply the years of tissue damage from elevated sugar levels. And since most diabetics don't want to give themselves injections, physicians use oral medications to delay the day of the needle.

In many ways it would be better to use insulin injections from the beginning and avoid the side effects of the oral medications. In fact, many of the medications used simply force the pancreas to produce even more insulin—so the result would be the same if one took injections and at the same time avoided side effects! However, there are now additional classes of oral medications that work in other ways than chemically forcing the pancreas to produce more insulin. They cooperate with the body's effort to make more sugar movers. But they are expensive and still have side effects.

How much better to influence the body to make sugar movers naturally, rather than continuing to increase blood levels of insulin! And that is the effect of exercise. Using our muscles has the effect of actually changing our genes (DNA) or the chemicals controlling what the DNA does. The result is the increasing production of sugar movers.

So, since the problem is the lack of sugar movers and since the only way to increase those naturally is to exercise—walk, walk, walk, and use only plant sources of food. Even if you don't get completely well (normal sugar without medication), you will be so close to being well that likely a very small amount of medication will keep your sugar at safe levels!

It is critical that someone with type 2 diabetes who "gets well" on the plan recommended here must stay with it religiously. They are not cured but are, if you will, in remission. Returning to the old lifestyle will likely plunge them into diabetes again. (Don't blame the physicians who look on this plan with some concern. They are the ones who have to struggle to get the diabetic back under control again when he/she falls back into the old ways—without realizing their sugar was again out of control and wreaking havoc in their bodies.)

Keep in mind that the effort it takes to get well works completely for only about 40 percent of diabetics, although the other 60 percent do extremely well. And the 40 percent must stay with the plan to stay well. If they become ill enough to be in the hospital, even while following the plan as well as they can while in bed, they will regress to needing diabetic medication again. Most of these can be well again once they are out of the hospital and back on the plan, but this illustrates how fragile a former diabetic's state is.

—Jim Brackett, M.A., M.P.H.

---

[1]Unless otherwise noted, "diabetes" refers to type 2, formerly called adult-onset. Only 10 percent of diabetes in the U.S. is type 1, which used to be called childhood-onset. Type 1 diabetes is a different disease, caused by some as-yet-unknown agent or circumstance that destroys the insulin-producing cells in the pancreas. Even among people or cultures that have a genetic predisposition to developing diabetes, type 2 rarely occurs if a healthy lifestyle is followed. In other words, genetics may load the diabetes gun but lifestyle pulls the trigger. In some cases of type 1 diabetes, if this lifestyle is followed shortly after the condition is diagnosed, the "honeymoon" has been extended for up to seven years. And even then, when insulin injections become necessary, if this exercise and plant food program is used, blood-sugar control will be much more successful. Type 1 diabetics, if they use insulin wisely, exercise, and eat plant foods, can stay well for a normal lifetime.

[2]We find that diabetics must walk four miles each day or they can't seem to get well. Many can exercise that much, but if they are overweight or over 35 years of age, they should talk to their physician about how quickly it would be safe for them to reach that distance. (Remember, it can be done in pieces throughout the day—it doesn't have to be four miles all at once!)

[3]Walnuts were the first nut to be studied. As time and funding allowed other nuts to be tested, the incidence of heart disease was again found to be lower. We now know that this effect is the result of certain "healthy" fats found in plant foods. The effect is greater (to a degree) when more of these plant fats are eaten, and since all nuts are higher in fat than most other plants, the result is more pronounced. However, all these were replacement studies. Nuts were not simply added to the diet; they replaced some other form of fat and calories. So we can't eat as before and then eat more nuts besides!

[4]Gluco translocators, or "sugar movers," move sugar from the blood into the cell.

[5]Insulin can't be taken by mouth to treat diabetes because it's a protein and would be broken down into amino acids before it could be absorbed into the bloodstream.

Breakfast Secrets

Granola

Muesli

Creamy
Rice

Welcome to the recipe section of this book. Here you'll find delicious ways of using the seven secrets in your cooking. Our philosophy for better health has been shaped by science, the Bible, and the practical counsel of a widely quoted health advocate from yesteryear: Ellen White. We hope the nuggets from these sources will inspire you as much as they have us!

MAPLE NUT GRANOLA

Most granola at the market tastes like oatmeal cookies! This delicious recipe, without refined fat, will be a real hit if you carefully follow the directions. With experience, it will be oven-ready in 15 minutes.

- 1 cup water
- ½ cup honey
- 1 tablespoon molasses, optional
- 1 tablespoon vanilla
- 1 teaspoon maple flavoring
- 1 teaspoon salt
- 2 cups pitted dates
- 1 cup walnuts, Brazil nuts, peanuts, or almonds
- 13 cups old-fashioned oats (42-ounce carton Quaker Oats)
- 1-2 cups quick oats, if needed
- ½ cup shredded, unsweetened coconut, optional
- 1-2 cups coarsely chopped walnuts, pecans, almonds, or peanuts

1. Put water, honey, flavorings, dates, and 1 cup nuts in blender. Blend for about 1 minute until smooth.

This becomes quite thick, and you may need to help it blend by carefully stirring from the top with a rubber spatula while it blends.

2. Place oats and remaining ingredients (except quick oats) in a large mixing bowl. Add blended mix to the oats and gently mix together with your hands.

Keep tossing until all the oats look moist and there are no dry, whitish-colored oat flakes in the mix. Avoid the temptation to squeeze or knead the mix with your hands. You want to retain the shape of the oat flakes without pulverizing them. Plastic food-handling gloves are a great help.

3. If the mix is too wet, the finished granola will not be tender. If it is sticking to your hands or feels sticky, add the extra quick oats and work them into the mix.

If you are using gloves, it will be the right consistency when it hardly sticks at all. I almost always need the extra oatmeal along with the 42-ounce carton of oats, but ingredients can vary, and experience will help you get the right balance of moisture every time.

If your finished granola is hard and tough, you got it too wet. It is just right when there are some clumps that break apart easily, but it is not all powdery and dry.

4. Place mixture in two large cake pans or sheet pans that have sides, taking care not to pack or pat it down tightly. Keep it light and airy.

5. Place pans in oven at 175°F for about 8 hours—no need to stir if it is baked slowly. If the temperature is too high, it will become dark brown or burned on top and uncooked underneath. When the uncooked part dries out, it will be tough and hard. Longer, slower cooking will result in an even, golden-brown product.

The right temperature is critical, so err on the low side or check it with an oven thermometer, since ovens vary greatly. A convection oven will usually give a more tender result.

🍂*Makes about 24 cups.*

CREAMY RICE CEREAL

This recipe became a favorite of ours when we worked in the Caribbean. Another way the islanders make their "porridge" is by preparing a thin cornmeal mush containing coconut milk.

- 1 cup coconut milk or soy milk
- 1 banana
- 1 cup pineapple juice
- ½ teaspoon coconut extract
- 4 cups cooked rice
- crushed pineapple and raisins

1. Blend together the coconut or soy milk, banana, juice, and coconut extract.

2. Place rice in a casserole dish that has been lightly coated with oil, and fold in the crushed pineapple and raisins. Stir in the blended milk and juice.

3. Bake at 350°F about 20 minutes until hot enough to serve, or about 8 minutes in the microwave.

🍂*Makes 6 cups.*

MUESLI FOR ONE

Here's a delicious one-person recipe for that favorite Scandinavian breakfast. Multiply according to the number served, but keep in mind that this makes a very generous serving—about 2 cups.

- ½ cup old-fashioned oats
- ¼ cup diced dried fruit (apricots, dates, and dried cranberries are good together)
- 1 cup soy milk (or piña colada juice) with a few slices of banana blended in
- ½ cup diced fresh apple
- 1 tablespoon chopped nuts
- pinch of orange zest (optional)

1. Place oats in a dry pan over medium-high heat and stir until just beginning to lightly brown.

2. Pour toasted oats into a bowl and add dried fruit and milk (or juice). Let sit overnight in refrigerator.

3. In the morning, add as desired: diced apple, chopped nuts, sliced bananas or peaches, grapes, berries, or other fruits. Add more milk or juice if desired. Serve cold or at room temperature.

🍂*Makes 2 cups.*

Light and Tender Waffles

Fruit Sauce

We have tried many combinations of waffle ingredients and made thousands of waffles. When we learned about the antioxidant benefits of flaxseed, we tried it in waffles. Our daughter Kimberley developed this recipe, which seems to have just the right combination of ingredients. It surpasses anything we have tried yet. We were surprised to discover that the flax works like leavening, causing the batter to bubble up and fill all the depressions in the waffle iron.

LIGHT AND TENDER WAFFLES

2 cups water

1 tablespoon concentrated apple juice*

1 cup quick oats

¼ cup millet or cornmeal

¼ cup flaxseed

¼ cup **raw cashew nuts**

2 tablespoons cornstarch (optional) (helps waffle keep its shape when cool)

½ teaspoon salt

*Makes waffle brown; 1 date or ½ tablespoon of raisins may be used instead.

1. Preheat waffle iron.

If your iron is old and worn, you probably have to use plenty of nonstick spray. The new waffle irons are not expensive, and a new Teflon surface stays nice a long time if you never grease or wash it. The nonstick sprays leave a residue that builds up, making the waffles stick. So don't spray, and get a nicer-appearing waffle as well!

2. Blend all ingredients for 1 minute.

3. Pour mixture into preheated waffle iron and close the lid. Bake until steam stops rising and the waffle is golden brown and crisp.

Hint: We've found that the time to bake these waffles varies greatly with the particular waffle iron—from 4 to 12 minutes. So follow the steam rule above, and you won't have a sticky mess! Once you know how long your iron takes, it's simpler to use a timer than watch the steam.

4. Remove to a cooling rack and serve.

Don't stack waffles when they're hot, or they'll become soggy and compressed. Use a toaster to add crispiness and reheat leftovers.

Serving Tips: Delicious with a warm fruit sauce (blueberry, apricot, or cherry) or sliced fresh peaches. For something really special, try adding a scoop of Five Loaves Rice Cream or Whipped Topping (p. 99). Also delicious with Simple Butter (p. 56) and Maple Syrup Sauce (p. 19).

Special Hint: An ordinary fruit sauce will look silky-smooth if the right thickening agent is used. Refrigerated fruit sauce made from potato starch or Clear Jel keeps its creamy texture instead of jelling.

Makes 1½-2 large waffles (6-8 squares). Works good in Belgian waffle irons, too.

Five Loaves Rice Cream

FRUIT SAUCE

4 cups diced fresh or frozen fruit (blueberries, blackberries, apricots, peaches, cherries, apples, or pears are good)

12-ounce can frozen concentrated apple or white grape juice

1 cup water

3 tablespoons potato starch or ¼ cup **Clear Jel** dissolved in ½ cup water (⅓ cup cornstarch may be used instead)

1. Place fruit, juice, and water in a saucepan. Place over high heat until mixture begins to boil.

With apples, turn down heat and simmer until apples are soft (5-10 minutes).

2. Remove from heat and stir in dissolved starch. Return to heat and stir until it just begins to boil and becomes thick.

Hint: Add the dissolved starch slowly and stir briskly to prevent lumps from forming. As you add and stir, the sauce will immediately thicken. Stop adding starch when the mixture reaches the desired consistency. Some tart fruits may need more sweetening. This may be done by adding a little honey or other sweetener of choice.

≈Makes about 6 cups.

FIVE LOAVES RICE CREAM

Pictured above; recipe on page 99.

"Grains, fruits, nuts, and vegetables constitute the diet chosen for us by our Creator. These foods, prepared in as simple and natural a manner as possible, are the most healthful and nourishing. They impart a strength, a power of endurance, and a vigor of intellect that are not afforded by a more complex and stimulating diet."

E. G. White, The Ministry of Healing, *p. 296*

French Toast

Crepes

SIMPLE FRENCH TOAST

1 cup orange juice (not concentrated)

⅓ cup flour (may use whole wheat, but white flour will give a nicer appearance)

6 or 7 slices whole wheat bread

1. Place orange juice and flour in a bowl and stir briskly with a wire whip.

2. Dip bread, one slice at a time, and place in a preheated nonstick skillet (medium heat). Gently press the bread with a spatula so that all of it contacts the griddle. This will help it to brown evenly. Turn over after 1-2 minutes.

Serving Tip: Use date-nut or raisin bread and serve with almond butter, topped with apricot or pear sauce. Or spread French toast with peanut butter and top with hot applesauce or a bit of Maple Syrup Sauce (p. 19).

☙*Serves 2-3.*

FRENCH CREPES

1½ cups water

¼ cup raw cashew nuts (may use 1½ cups soy milk instead of water and cashew nuts)

½ cup quick oats

½ cup whole wheat or brown rice flour

1 tablespoon apple juice concentrate or ½ tablespoon honey

½ teaspoon salt

½ cup tofu (optional) (makes the crepes richer and more tender)

1. Blend ingredients together about 1 minute.

2. Lift preheated nonstick skillet from burner and pour ¼ cup portion, tipping in a circular motion so crepe flows large and thin. Use medium-high temperature until dry on top (about 1 minute), then loosen gently with spatula and turn, cooking the other side for about 30 seconds. Stack finished crepes on a flat plate and cover with a cloth to keep warm.

You can make these ahead and refrigerate, wrapping a plate of stacked crepes in a plastic bag. Warm in microwave before serving.

Serving Tip: Place a thin layer of sugarless jam on crepe and then spread across the middle a spoonful of Whipped Topping (p. 99). Roll up and drizzle with Maple Syrup Sauce (p. 19) if desired.

☙*Makes 12 crepes.*

WHOLE GRAIN CEREAL

This cereal is wholesome and hearty—just whole grains. It is quick and simple to make overnight in a small Crock-Pot. Make it special by adding dates and raisins. Serve with dry-roasted peanuts for extra crunch. Make ahead and freeze in smaller amounts for handy use in the morning.

½ cup whole rye or wheat

½ cup brown rice, barley, millet, or mixed whole rice

3 cups boiling water

½ teaspoon salt

1 cup raisins and chopped dates (optional)

Crock-Pot Method: Place all the grains in a Crock-Pot and add the boiling water and salt. Let cook 8 hours and serve.

Hint: If you like the cereal less creamy or starchy, you can wait to add the rice, barley, or millet about 1½ hours before serving. I like to use rye and put it in the Crock-Pot at bedtime. Since I am an early riser, I wait to add the rice or softer grains when I get up, about 1½ hours before breakfast. Then about 15 minutes before breakfast I add the raisins and dates. Good served with sliced bananas, apples, pears, or peaches.

Stove Top Method: Place 3 cups water in a kettle along with rye or wheat and salt. Simmer for 1 hour. Then add the rice or softer grain and continue cooking until water is gone—about 45 minutes. Just before it has finished cooking, add the raisins and dates if desired.

FRESH FRUIT SAUCE

2 cups fresh or frozen fruit (peaches, pears, mangos, strawberries, blackberries, or raspberries)

honey or other sweetener of choice

1. Peel and cut the fruit into small pieces.

2. Place fruit in a food processor and add sweetener. Secure top and pulse several times to coarsely chop the fruit. Serve on waffles, French toast, crepes, or shortcake with Whipped Topping (p. 99) or Five Loaves Rice Cream (p. 99).

☙*Makes 2 cups.*

Though eggs have a tradition in cooking and baking, we have not used them in our recipes. You can make light muffins, pancakes, and waffles and even crepes without them! You might notice a slight difference in taste and texture, but most of our restaurant customers didn't miss them at all. So just to round out our breakfast section, we include some delicious replacements for egg and hash brown fans without the usual cholesterol or grease.

MAPLE SYRUP SAUCE

1. Dissolve 1 tablespoon cornstarch in ¼ cup water.

2. Dilute 1 cup pure maple syrup with 1 cup water. Bring to a boil and slowly stir in the dissolved cornstarch. Serve over crepes, waffles, or pancakes.

☙*Makes 2 cups.*

WHOLE WHEAT PANCAKES

2 cups whole wheat pastry flour

1 teaspoon salt

2 cups soy milk or nut milk

2 tablespoons honey

2 tablespoons **Ener-G Baking Powder** (or 1 tablespoon regular baking powder)

1. Blend all ingredients together in a blender or with a wire whip.

2. Pour onto hot griddle, being careful not to stir down the bubbles (no bubbles with regular baking powder). Bake until golden brown on each side.

Variation: *Add 1 mashed banana or 1 cup blueberries. Other flours may be used instead of whole wheat, such as rice, barley, corn, or oat flour.*

See Efficiency Tips (p. 101) for homemade pancake mix.

☙*Makes 8-10 pancakes.*

Scottish Oat Cakes

Dried Fruit Sauce

SCOTTISH OAT CAKES

This is a delicious make-ahead treat.

- ¼ cup whole wheat pastry flour
- 1 cup Brazil nuts (or walnuts)
- 1 cup quick oats
- 1 teaspoon salt
- ¼ cup honey, warmed

1. Place flour and nuts in a food processor and whiz for 1 minute or until nuts are as fine as the flour but not getting buttery or sticking to the sides. Pour into a mixing bowl and add oats and salt. Stir in warmed honey until a ball of dough forms, adding a little water if needed. Mixture should stick together, but not be so wet that it sticks to your hands.

2. Divide into about 12 walnut-sized balls and place on two nonstick cookie sheets. Roll thin with a rolling pin.

If the pan sides are deep, turn it upside down and make your cakes on the bottom in order to roll the cakes flat with a rolling pin. Cover them with plastic wrap to keep the roller from sticking.

3. Bake 10-12 minutes at 350°F. Watch carefully—they burn easily!

4. Serve with thickened fruit topping such as blueberry, cherry, or peach. Add nut or soy milk if desired.

🍂*Makes 1 dozen.*

DRIED FRUIT SAUCE

- 1 apple, diced small
- 1 cup crushed pineapple
- ½ cup orange juice (not concentrate)
- ¼ cup pure maple syrup or honey (optional)
- 1 teaspoon vanilla
- ½ teaspoon coconut extract
- ¼ teaspoon salt
- 1 cup water
- ½ cup dried apricots, diced
- ½ cup dried prunes, diced
- ¼ cup dried cherries (optional)
- 1 tablespoon cornstarch dissolved in ¼ cup water

1. Place all ingredients except dissolved cornstarch in a saucepan. Bring to a boil and then reduce heat to low and simmer for 20 minutes. Stir in dissolved cornstarch to thicken as desired. (Omit this step if the sauce is as thick as you like without it.) Serve over Scottish Oat Cakes (p. 21) or whole wheat toast.

Tip: Great for camping trips. Dried fruit (including apple) can be diced and placed in a plastic bag. Even omit sweeteners—the simple flavors of the dried fruits stewed together will be enjoyed by all.

Preserving Tip: This sauce may be preserved by hot-pack canning. Simply place jars in a microwave with 1 inch of water in each jar for 10 minutes. Boil the metal lid seals in a small pan of water for 1 minute. Empty the water out of the jars and pour the boiling sauce into the jars. Screw on the lids right away and let sit to cool and seal.

🍂*Makes 1 quart.*

VIENNESE APPLE COFFEE CAKE

Pictued below; recipe on page 23.

Mocha Carob Drink

FRITTATA

½ cup chopped onion

¼ cup diced pepper (green, red, or yellow)

1 clove garlic, minced

1 small zucchini

1 cup firm tofu (7-8 ounces)

¼ cup water (omit if soft tofu is used)

½ teaspoon salt or butter-flavored salt

1 teaspoon food yeast flakes

1 teaspoon Bragg Liquid Aminos

1 tablespoon cornstarch

1 tablespoon fine cornmeal or corn flour

1. Simmer onion, peppers, and garlic in 2 tablespoons of water for 5 minutes. Add sliced zucchini and cook 3 more minutes. Remove from heat. Place a shallow, nonstick 8-inch skillet (or frittata pan) on the burner at medium-low heat to preheat.

2. Place tofu and remaining ingredients in blender and blend—not necessarily smooth but thick.

3. Stir blended tofu into the onion mixture and pour into the preheated skillet, smoothing the surface. Cook for 15 minutes or until the frittata is almost set. Cover handle with foil or slip frittata onto a cookie sheet and place under broiler for about 2 minutes or until the top is set and golden. Allow the frittata to stand for 5 minutes before cutting into wedges for serving.

Makes one 8-inch frittata.

MOCHA CAROB DRINK

Want a morning hot drink without caffeine? This one will make you think you're sipping a latte!

1 cup soy milk

½ teaspoon carob powder

½ teaspoon **Roma** or coffee substitute of choice

½ tablespoon honey

¼ teaspoon almond extract

¼ teaspoon vanilla

Blend briefly on low, or mix until all is dissolved. Heat and serve hot or cold.

Makes 1 cup.

Frittata

Scoop into muffin top pan. Or using an ice-cream scoop, place six mounds of batter on a cookie sheet. Briskly rap the cookie sheet on the counter several times, and the mounds will spread into flat circles.

5. Place in 400°F oven; bake for 15-20 minutes or until golden brown on top and bottom. See Create-a-Cake (p. 79) for more muffin ideas.

Makes 8 muffin tops.

VIENNESE APPLE COFFEE CAKE

(See picture, page 21.) This is a rich pastry—use sparingly. Dough can be used as shortcake or scones (p. 79).

Filling:
2 apples, peeled and thinly sliced

⅔ cup apple juice concentrate

½ teaspoon coriander (or cinnamon)

¼ teaspoon cardamom (optional)

1½ tablespoons Clear Jel or cornstarch dissolved in 3 tablespoons water

Topping:
½ cup quick oats or white flour

½ cup whole wheat flour

½ teaspoon salt (or Flavacol)

½ cup Brazil nuts or unsweetened coconut

¼ cup brown sugar and 2 tablespoons water or 3 tablespoons warmed honey

Dough:
1¾ cups whole wheat flour (part white OK)

1½ cups coconut or soy milk (or ½ cup each water and coconut milk for less-rich version)

½ cup sugar

1½ tablespoons Ener-G Baking Powder

½ teaspoon salt

1. Bring apples, juice, and coriander to a boil and simmer two mintes. Stir in dissolved Clear Jel. Turn off heat.

2. Blend topping ingredients in food processor 1 minute. Add water or honey. Pulse to moisten crumbs.

3. Mix ingredients for dough. It should be stiff and sticky. Lightly oil a 9" x 13" pan. Using a rubber spatula, spread dough over the bottom of the pan.

4. Arrange apple filling over the batter. Sprinkle crumb topping over filling. Bake in preheated oven at 350°F for 30-35 minutes or until knife inserted in the center comes out clean.

Makes 12 servings.

BANANA DATE-NUT MUFFIN TOPS

Muffin tops are always my favorite part of the muffin—slightly crisp on top and easier to spread with butter or jam. So just make a trayful of tops! You can buy special muffin top pans, or just use a cookie sheet. We've kept the recipe small because they are so good fresh from the oven; if you want to double the recipe extras can be frozen .

1 cup whole wheat flour

1 tablespoon Ener-G Baking Powder or 2 teaspoons regular baking powder

½ teaspoon salt

scant ½ cup Brazil nuts or walnuts

½ cup walnuts

½ cup chopped dates

1 medium banana

¼ cup honey

¼ cup or more soy milk (may use water)

1. Preheat oven to 400°F and prepare muffin top pan or cookie sheet by coating lightly with oil—or line the cookie sheet with a Bake Magic baking sheet.

2. Place flour, baking powder, salt, and Brazil nuts in a food processor and process together for 1 minute, until the nuts are as fine as the flour. Add walnuts and blend a few seconds to chop the nuts coarsely.

3. Mash the bananas with a fork and place in a 2-cup measuring cup along with the honey. Add soy milk to make a total of 1 cup mixture with the bananas and honey. Stir together.

4. Place flour mixture in a mixing bowl. Add dates and banana mixture, and stir briskly until well mixed. Scoop into muffin top pan. Or using

TOFU SCRAMBLE WITH VEGETABLES

This tofu recipe is especially good when the tofu is served moist, with the vegetables not overcooked to preserve their bright colors.

- 1 16-ounce brick firm tofu
- 1-2 cloves garlic, pressed
- 1 teaspoon butter-flavored salt
- 2 teaspoons Bragg Liquid Aminos
- ¼ teaspoon turmeric
- 4 fresh mushrooms, sliced, or 1 small zucchini, diced
- 3 green onions, chopped
- 1 small tomato, diced

1. Crumble tofu into a nonstick skillet and add garlic, salt, Bragg's, and turmeric.

Cook covered 10 minutes (medium-high).

Hint: For a more scrambled egg look and texture, don't stir as you would eggs, or the result will be crumbly. Simply turn once or twice.

2. Add zucchini or mushrooms and cook uncovered for 5 minutes. Add green onions and cook about 1 minute. Remove from heat and add the tomato.

Variation: *For a simple scrambled tofu, leave out the vegetables. Cook until most of the moisture is evaporated and the tofu resembles scrambled eggs. Or bake uncovered in a lightly oiled casserole dish (include vegetables if desired) at 350°F for 45 minutes or until it sets up. See page 101 for a tofu seasoning mix.*

Serves 4.

Tofu Scramble

Oven Hash
Browns

OVEN HASH BROWNS

¾ cup water

½ cup raw cashew nuts

½ tablespoon onion powder

½ teaspoon garlic powder

2 tablespoons Chicken-Like Seasoning

½ cup finely diced onion (optional)

2 pounds frozen shredded hash browns (about 8 cups)

May use purchased frozen potatoes, but make sure they are free of hydrogenated oils. If you make them from home-cooked potatoes, it works best if potatoes are slightly undercooked.

1. Blend cashews and water with seasonings for at least 1 minute until smooth. (May use 1 cup coconut milk instead.)

2. Pour over potatoes and add the diced onion. Mix well with hands to coat all the potatoes. (May freeze some of the uncooked mix for future use.)

3. Place on a nonstick or lightly oiled cookie sheet and place on bottom rack of unheated oven. Turn on the oven to 400°F and bake for 20-30 minutes until golden brown on the edges and lightly browned in places on the bottom. Don't overbake, or they will become dry.

4. Pile in a serving dish to retain some of the moisture and serve. The serving dish may be covered and placed in a warm oven. Don't leave them warming for more than 30 minutes—they will begin to discolor.

Variation: *These potatoes can be made into patties before baking. Just form into patties on a cookie sheet instead of spreading them out, and bake the same as Oven Hash Browns. Remove from oven when patties are golden brown on the bottom.*

❧*Makes 8 cups.*

Take a look at the long aisles of prepared foods in your supermarket. There are many that contain no meat—it's a new day for a healthier cuisine and vegetarian choices! But one after another list such items as cheese, milk, buttermilk, mono- and diglycerides, partially hydrogenated oils, butterfat, etc.

When Darryl came to work at Five Loaves, he was faced with some new challenges. He had recently become a vegetarian. Preparing dishes rich in meat and refined foods became such a struggle that he finally resigned his former job and came to our little restaurant and tried to prepare appetizing dishes in a new way.

I noticed he struggled to make sauces for creamy entrées and soups. We didn't have his favorite ingredients to "tighten" the sauce—butter, oil, milk, cream, and different kinds of cheese. But the Lord blessed his efforts, and his experience as a chef made him a quick learner. Soon he was making flavor-filled dishes with our basic sauce and his own special flair. He was delighted to learn about a kind of cornstarch we used called Clear Jel. It's made from waxy corn and makes a silkier, creamier sauce that doesn't separate and change texture in the refrigerator. See page 103 for where to find it.

In this section we'll show how you can still enjoy such favorites as creamed soups, macaroni and cheese, pizza, and much more—all possible if you learn this basic skill. "It's in the sauce." Once you learn how to make this Basic Cream Sauce, the door will be opened for you to make an endless variety of favorite foods.

BASIC CREAM SAUCE

Pay special attention to steps 1 and 2—this is the key to blending a sauce with an authentic look and feel. Many cooks fail here—they don't blend the mixture long enough. The result is a somewhat gritty or grainy texture. Blend nuts with a small amount of water—enough to submerge them. A thicker mixture results and will become smooth more quickly. Then add the rest of the water in the recipe. This is why, in many of our recipes, some water is added while blending and then more is added later.

- 1 cup raw cashew nuts
- 2 cups water
- 1 teaspoon salt or more to taste
- 2 teaspoons onion powder
- 1 tablespoon Chicken-Like Seasoning (or 1 tablespoon food yeast flakes and ½ teaspoon more salt)
- ½ teaspoon garlic powder (optional)
- 2 tablespoons cornstarch, flour, or Clear Jel
- 1½ cups more water (to be added after blending)

1. Place all ingredients in blender and blend on high for about 2 minutes until smooth.

2. When the mixture is so smooth that no graininess is felt in a drop of it between your thumb and finger, pour into a saucepan. Add the 1½ cups more water to the blender, swish it around, and add to the mixture in the pan. Bring to a boil, stirring constantly as it thickens to keep it from lumping. As soon as it thickens, remove from heat.

3. If a thicker sauce is needed, return to heat and slowly stir in more starch that has been dissolved in cold water, letting it come to a gentle boil as it thickens.

❧Makes 4 cups.

See pages 106 and 107 for more information on the use of starches and substitutions to use in making nondairy sauces.

SOY CREAM SAUCE

Replace cashew nuts with 1 cup soaked soybeans or 1½ cups tofu, or use 3 cups plain, unsweetened soy milk. Add water to make 4 cups total mixture.

COCONUT CREAM SAUCE

Replace cashew nuts with 1 can (scant 2 cups) coconut milk (or, for a lighter sauce, 1 cup coconut milk) and add water to make 4 cups total mixture.

Other nuts can sometimes be used in place of cashews, such as almonds, peanuts, or Brazil nuts. The flavor and texture will be affected according to the nut used.

SIMPLE GRAVY

This is a variation of the Basic Cream Sauce, with a rich, meaty flavor.

- 1 cup raw cashew nuts
- ½ teaspoon salt (or more to taste)
- 2 teaspoons onion powder
- ¼ teaspoon garlic powder
- 1 tablespoon Chicken-Like or Beef-Like Seasoning
- 1 tablespoon Bragg Liquid Aminos or soy sauce (omit for chickenlike gravy)
- 1 tablespoon food yeast flakes
- 3 tablespoons flour or 2 tablespoons cornstarch (I like flour better for gravy)
- 4-ounce can mushrooms after blending, or blend for 1 second just to chop coarsely (optional)
- water to make 4 cups total mixture

Follow directions under Basic Cream Sauce (p. 26)

Lite Gravy Option: Use ½ cup cashew nuts.

Peanut Gravy Option: Use ¾ cup dry-roasted peanuts and 1 can garbanzos, using same ingredients as in Simple Gravy, and adding water to equal 4 total cups gravy. May omit salt.

SIMPLE CHEESE SAUCE

- 1 cup raw cashew nuts
- 2 cups water
- ½ large or 1 small red bell pepper (or ¼ cup canned pimentos or red peppers)
- 1½ teaspoons salt
- 2 teaspoons onion powder
- 2 tablespoons food yeast flakes (optional)
- ½ teaspoon garlic powder

Blend smooth (about 2 minutes) and then bring to a boil, stirring until thick. Use for pizza, lasagna, burritos, etc.

Lite Cheese Option: Use only ½ cup cashew nuts plus 1 tablespoon cornstarch.

❧Makes 3 cups.

Secrets for Sauces and Creams

Creamed Asparagus

CREAMED ASPARAGUS

In the spring when asparagus is available we serve Creamed Asparagus over rice or toast as often as possible. It's definitely one of our family favorites and never fails to get compliments from our guests.

2 cups fresh asparagus, cut in 1-inch pieces (or use whole as pictured)

1 medium onion

½ cup diced red pepper or ¼ cup diced pimiento

1 cup sliced fresh or canned mushrooms, or 1 cup diced **Veggie Cutlets** (p. 37)

1 recipe **Basic Cream Sauce** (p. 26)

1. Simmer asparagus, onions, peppers, mushrooms, and seasonings together until tender—add small amount of water as needed.

2. Set steamed vegetables aside, reserving any of the liquid left from cooking them and using it as some of the water when blending the cream sauce.

3. Make Basic Cream Sauce and stir in the steamed vegetables after it has thickened. Serve hot over rice or whole wheat toast.

❧*Makes 8 cups.*

À LA KING SUPREME

Here's a variation of the Creamed Asparagus (p. 27) that you can use when asparagus is not in season:

1 medium onion, diced

½ cup diced red sweet pepper

½ cup sliced canned mushrooms

½ teaspoon salt

1 cup frozen peas

1½ cups cooked or canned garbanzo beans

½ cup water chestnuts (optional)

1 recipe **Basic Cream Sauce** (p. 26)

1. Simmer onion, pepper, mushrooms, and salt in a small amount of water until vegetables are tender. Add peas and garbanzos (including liquid if using canned garbanzos). Gently mix together and then strain off and reserve the liquid to use as part of the water in the cream sauce.

2. Make Basic Cream Sauce and add vegetables. Serve hot over brown rice or pasta.

❧*Makes 8 cups.*

Making healthy choices reminds me of a classic quote we have been sharing from the pen of that inspired writer on health more than 100 years ago. I like her philosophy!

"Those who take an extreme view of health reform are in danger of preparing tasteless dishes, making them so insipid that they are not satisfying. Food should be prepared in such a way that it will be appetizing as well as nourishing. It should not be robbed of that which the system needs. I use some salt, and always have, because salt, instead of being deleterious, is actually essential for the blood. Vegetables should be made palatable with a little milk or cream, or something equivalent."

E. G. White, Counsels on Health, *p. 136*

Crusty Potpie

Here's an entrée that requires more time to make, but is worth the effort. Make it a day ahead and warm in the oven before serving—a good special-occasion entrée. This is a favorite entrée when I have guests who are not vegetarians. It seems to satisfy any kind of appetite and always receives compliments.

CRUSTY POTPIE

2½ cups diced potatoes

1½ cups sliced carrots

1 cup diced onion

1½ cups frozen peas or green beans

1 cup diced Veggie Cutlets (p. 37)

½ teaspoon salt

1 recipe Basic Cream Sauce (p. 26)

double recipe Cobbler Crust (p. 88)

1. Simmer vegetables (except peas) and diced cutlets in a small amount of water and salt until barely tender. Drain and place in a 9" x 13" dish that has been lightly oiled around the top edge. Scatter frozen peas on top of the vegetables.

2. Make Basic Cream Sauce. Add water to make 5 cups. Pour over the vegetables. (Use plenty of sauce—a ratio of about half vegetables and half sauce.)

3. Make Cobbler Crust and roll into a rectangle ¼ inch thick and place on vegetables (to transfer, fold twice—then unfold in dish). This dough uses yeast, so it will need to rise for 45 minutes until double. Or make Simple and Flaky Piecrust (p. 83). (No need to let this one rise!)

4. Bake at 350°F for about 25 minutes, until crust is golden brown.

Tip: If you plan to serve this the next day, let it cool completely before covering. Then place the whole casserole in a plastic bag and refrigerate. (Otherwise, the crust is likely to wrinkle a bit, though it doesn't hurt the taste!) Remove cover and place in 350°F oven to heat before serving. A piece of foil may be placed loosely over the top if it begins to brown too much.

CREAMY RICE CASSEROLE

My friend Marilyn Kelln gave me this recipe. She likes to use it for guests who are not vegetarian. It isn't one they will compare with a favorite meat dish—it's delicious and stands on its own merits.

½ cup sliced almonds

4-ounce can mushroom pieces, drained

2 cups celery or broccoli, diced small

2 bunches green onions, chopped

½ cup green pepper, diced

½ cup water

1 teaspoon salt

1½ cups (14 ounces) tofu

½ cup cashew nuts

1 cup water

¼ cup mayonnaise of choice

1 tablespoon Beef-Like Seasoning

2 tablespoons Bragg Liquid Aminos or soy sauce

4-5 cups cooked rice (1½ cups uncooked)

8-ounce can sliced water chestnuts

2 tablespoons dried parsley flakes

1 cup diced Veggie Cutlets (p. 37) (may omit, or use diced, canned soymeat or gluten steaks)

3 slices bread, cubed

1. Heat a nonstick skillet over medium to high temperature. Add sliced almonds and stir while they toast or turn golden brown. Remove to a separate container.

2. Place mushrooms, celery, onions, and green pepper in the skillet with ½ cup water and 1 teaspoon salt. Simmer for about 8 minutes. (If using broccoli, add after onions and peppers have cooked 5 minutes. Then simmer 2 or 3 minutes.)

3. Blend the tofu, cashew nuts, water, mayonnaise, and seasonings until smooth. Stir into the celery and onion mixture.

4. Lightly oil a 9" x 13" casserole dish, and fill with cooked rice—about half full. Cover with the blended mixture, and sprinkle with water chestnuts, parsley flakes, diced cutlets, and sliced almonds. Then top with the bread cubes.

5. Bake uncovered at 350°F for 30-40 minutes until heated through and bread topping is crisp.

Serves 6-8.

CREAMY STROGANOFF

This recipe is an example of how cashew nuts can be blended with tofu to make an even richer, creamier sauce. It uses Veggie Cutlets *(p. 37) for the "meat." People always like it and ask for the recipe. The Island Stroganoff variation uses coconut milk and comes from our daughter Kathy, who lived in the Cayman Islands.*

⅓ cup cashew nuts

1 cup tofu

1 cup water

2 tablespoons Bragg Liquid Aminos

2 tablespoons Beef-Like Seasoning

2 tablespoons onion powder

3 tablespoons yeast flakes

2 cups water

1 onion, sliced into thin strips

1 cup or more canned mushrooms, or 2 cups fresh, sliced mushrooms

2 cups Veggie Cutlets (p. 37) cut or torn into pieces (canned gluten pieces such as Worthington Skallops may be used)

1. Place cashews and tofu in blender with 1 cup water; blend until smooth.

2. While blending, add seasonings and then the remaining 2 cups water after blend is smooth.

3. Meanwhile, sauté onions and mushrooms in a small amount of water until tender. Stir in the blended tofu mixture and the gluten pieces. Heat to serving temperature; do not boil, or the texture may become slightly curdled.

4. Serve over brown rice or pasta.

Variation: *Island Stroganoff Replace cashew nuts, tofu, and water with 1 can coconut milk; omit yeast flakes and add ½ teaspoon thyme.*

🍃*Makes 7 cups.*

PASTA PRIMAVERA

2 cups or more lightly steamed vegetables such as broccoli, spinach, cauliflower, carrots, onions, red or green peppers, and fresh or canned mushrooms

Note: The 2 cups measure is after cooking. This would be about 4 cups of raw vegetables.

1 recipe Basic Cream Sauce (p. 26) or Simple Cheese Sauce (p. 26)

2 cups Marinated Baked Tofu (p. 39) (optional)

4 cups cooked whole-grain pasta (approximately 2 cups uncooked)

Hint: Use an interestingly shaped pasta such as curly vegetable pasta or shells, spirals, or bows. See glossary (p. 105).

1. Boil and drain pasta according to package directions.

2. Steam vegetables in a small amount of salted water and set aside.

3. Make Basic Cream Sauce or Cheese Sauce and fold into the cooked pasta and steamed vegetables.

4. May be served immediately or placed in a casserole dish and sprinkled with seasoned bread crumbs and baked in a 350°F oven until topping browns.

🍃*Serves 6-8.*

> **"Those who entertain visitors, should have wholesome, nutritious food, from fruits, grains, and vegetables, prepared in a simple, tasteful manner. Such cooking will require but little extra labor or expense, and, partaken of in moderate quantities, will not injure any one."**
>
> *E. G. White,* Counsels on Diet and Foods, *p. 89*

VEGETARIAN PIZZA

1 12-inch pizza crust (use **Cobbler Crust** [p. 88] or **Pizza Crust** [p. 65])

Pizza crusts keep well in the freezer; also try English muffins, Mediterranean flat bread, or pita bread.

¾ cup **Simple Cheese Sauce** (p. 26)

1 cup pasta sauce or 8-ounce can seasoned tomato sauce

¼ cup sliced olives

¼ cup mushrooms

1 cup finely diced onions, green, red, and yellow bell peppers, etc.

1 cup shredded white **Sliceable Cashew Cheese** (p. 73) or pine nuts (optional)

1. Spread pizza crust with 1 cup of Simple Cheese Sauce, covering entire surface. Spoon the pasta sauce over the cheese and swirl it gently into the cheese.

2. Scatter surface with mushrooms, olives, and vegetables of choice. Just before serving, bake at 350°F for about 10 minutes.

Hint: This can be assembled several hours or a day ahead and baked just before mealtime for a quick entrée. The assembled pizza freezes well, if desired.

Option: A nice finishing touch: sprinkle shredded white Sliceable Cashew Cheese or pine nuts over the top!

🍂*Makes one 12-inch pizza.*

MACARONI AND CHEESE

Kathy told us this was the best macaroni and cheese she had ever tasted, and when we tried it, we had to agree. Thank you, Miriam Taylor, for sharing your recipe with us.

3 cups dry macaroni (use whole grain pasta if possible [see p. 104])

1 can coconut milk

1¼ cups water

¼ cup yeast flakes

2 teaspoons salt

¼ cup raw cashew pieces

¼ cup pimentos

3 tablespoons lemon juice

"Using a macrobiotic diet emphasizing whole grains, vegetables, and legumes while avoiding dairy products and most meats, nine men with prostate cancer had an average survival of 228 months, compared to 72 months for a matched group of men using no special diet."

Journal of the American College of Nutrition 12 (1993): 209-226

"Let him who is struggling against the power of appetite look to the Savior in the wilderness of temptation. See Him in His agony upon the cross, as He exclaimed, 'I thirst.' He has endured all that it is possible for us to bear. His victory is ours."

E. G. White, The Desire of Ages, p. 123

Tip: Another method for thickening a sauce uses a "puree." Examples of this are seen in Coconut Curry With Greens *(p. 33)* **and** Coconut Corn Chowder *(p. 70). Practice these recipes, and you will see that this is a secret worth learning. It has served me well many times when I needed a thicker sauce.*

¼ cup cornstarch

1 teaspoon onion powder

¼ cup **soy milk powder** (plain—not vanilla flavor) or increase cashews to ½ cup

1. Cook macaroni in 5 quarts boiling water with 2 teaspoons salt until soft. Follow package directions for whole grain pasta.

2. Meanwhile, blend remaining ingredients about 2 minutes until very smooth.

3. Drain cooked macaroni and return to kettle. Pour blended mixture into hot, drained macaroni and cook together until thick, stirring gently. Add 1-2 cups frozen peas or 1 cup mushrooms or sliced olives if desired.

4. Cover and let sit 5 or 10 minutes before serving, or put in an oiled casserole, cover with seasoned bread crumbs, and bake.

Tip: If made ahead and heated the next day, stir in some water before heating—it tends to dry if it sits.

⋐Serves 6-8.

The cheese sauce in this recipe may be replaced with Simple Cheese Sauce *(p. 26). After Simple Cheese Sauce has been blended, follow steps 3 and 4 above.*

Variation: *Lasagna and More*
You can see the potential for creating many dishes using Simple Cheese Sauce. You can adapt many of your favorite recipes using the cookbooks on your shelf. A classic example is everyone's favorite—lasagna. Using your favorite recipe, layer with pasta sauce, whole wheat lasagna, Spinach Filling *(p. 67) (double recipe), or other vegetables, instead of meat, and top with* Simple Cheese Sauce *(p. 26). A detailed recipe for lasagna can be found in* Best Gourmet Recipes, *p. 44.*

Thai-style Curry

Departing from the Basic Cream Sauce (p. 26) recipe, but still in the same category of creamy entrées, these two curry recipes will give you just the thing to cook up in a hurry and serve the heartiest of appetites.

Really Good THAI-STYLE CURRY

A favorite Thai ingredient is the peanut. This curry uses peanut butter to give it an inviting flavor and texture.

  1 cup diced carrots (optional if you don't have red or yellow peppers)

  1 onion, diced

  ½ cup each green and red peppers (yellow are nice too, if you have them)

  2 cloves garlic

  4-5 small zucchini or similar vegetable, diced small

  1 cup tomato sauce

  2 tablespoons peanut butter or ¼ cup dry-roasted peanuts

  2 tablespoons Bragg Liquid Aminos (or 1 tablespoon soy sauce)

  1 tablespoon Homemade Curry Powder (p. 33) (or other)

  ½ teaspoon or more salt to taste

  ½ cup fresh cilantro (optional)

  1 cup cooked garbanzos or lentils

  1 cup frozen peas

1. Place diced carrots, onion, peppers, and garlic (not the peas yet) in a kettle with a small amount of water and curry powder. Simmer about 5 minutes until tender.

2. Add zucchini, cover, and simmer 5 more minutes.

3. Blend all the remaining ingredients except the peas and garbanzos or lentils in a blender until smooth, and add to the cooked vegetables along with the frozen peas and garbanzos or lentils. Heat and serve over rice.

  Makes about 8 cups.

HOMEMADE CURRY POWDER

  2 tablespoons cumin

  2 tablespoons coriander

  2 teaspoons garlic powder

  2 teaspoons turmeric

  2 teaspoons fenugreek

  1 tablespoon California Chili (optional)

COCONUT CURRY WITH GREENS

  1 small onion, chopped

  2-3 cloves garlic, crushed

  1-inch piece of fresh ginger, grated or chopped fine

  1 teaspoon salt

  1-2 teaspoons Homemade Curry Powder (p. 33) (or other)

  1 medium sliced carrot

  2 cups chopped fresh greens (spinach, chard, beet greens, or kale) or 10-ounce package frozen chopped spinach, drained

  2 cups cooked or canned garbanzos or black beans or lentils

  14-ounce can petite diced tomatoes, drained

  1 can coconut milk

  1 cup golden raisins (optional)

1. Place onion, garlic, ginger, seasonings, and about ¼ cup water in a medium-sized kettle. Cover and simmer for 3 minutes.

2. Add the sliced carrot; cover and simmer for 5 more minutes.

3. Add the chopped greens and simmer 3 more minutes, adding a little more water if needed.

4. Add beans or lentils, tomatoes, curry powder, milk, and raisins. Heat and serve over rice.

If thicker curry is desired, place 1½ cups of the curry in blender and blend a few seconds to make a puree. Stir into the pot of curry and heat.

  Makes about 8 cups.

"In vegetarian populations it appears that nuts may be exerting the strongest protective effect [for coronary heart disease]. This was an unexpected finding, since it was anticipated that the absence of meat eating would be the dominant factor. When other population groups were examined similar findings became apparent, demonstrating a strong cardioprotective effect from nut ingestion approaching the level of effect seen with the use of lipid-lowering medication. It has been estimated that 1 ounce of daily nut ingestion may reduce the risk of fatal CHD by 45 percent when substituted for saturated fat and by 30 percent when substituted for carbohydrate intake.... Although nuts contain approximately 80 percent fat the nut feeding trials have not shown any associated weight gain in those ingesting nuts, suggesting the addition of nuts in the diet may have a satiating effect."

Asia Pacific Journal of Clinical Nutrition
13 (2004): S33

"God will cooperate with His children in preserving their health, if they eat with care, refusing to put unnecessary burdens on the stomach. He has graciously made the path of nature sure and safe, wide enough for all who walk in it. He has given for our sustenance the wholesome and health-giving productions of the earth."

E. G. White, Counsels on Diet and Foods, *p. 39*

Secrets to Replacing Meat in Your Favorite Recipes

hy vegetarian? The concept may seem extreme, considering that meat is a staple, and many would rather die younger than give up the best part of their day. That's easy to say until you are the widow of a 47-year-old heart attack victim. Was it really worth the beef? Of course, not all meat eaters die at 47. But today everyone knows that meat is high in cholesterol and the less of it you eat, the better off you'll be. The secret to success here is to replace it with something better that is also delicious. This key will unlock and offer alternatives for family favorites you thought you couldn't eat if you became a vegetarian.

OAT BURGER

This recipe replaces America's favorite fast food—the hamburger—and is an example of how grains and nuts can be combined to make delicious meatlike foods. Vegetarian burgers are readily available in many restaurants and supermarkets, but a careful look at the label is very revealing. Most are high in refined oils, and the few that are not are low in flavor. Here is an easy, cost-saving recipe you can make and freeze.

3 cups water

¼ cup Bragg Liquid Aminos or 2 tablespoons soy sauce

1 tablespoon Beef-Like Seasoning

1 teaspoon Wright's Hickory Seasoning (optional)

1 teaspoon Italian seasoning

1 teaspoon garlic powder

½ tablespoon onion powder

½ teaspoon salt

3 tablespoons food yeast flakes

¼ cup dry onion flakes or 1 onion, diced

3 cups quick oats or 2 cups quick oats and 1 cup bulgur wheat

½ cup ground walnuts or pecans

1. **Place all ingredients in a saucepan except oats and nuts; simmer together for 3 minutes. Remove from heat and stir in quick oats and nuts. Allow sufficient cooling to handle in next step.**

2. **Shape into burger-sized patties— use a half-cup ice-cream scoop if available— and place on a nonstick or Pam-sprayed cookie sheet.**

3. **Bake at 375°F until browned on both sides, or brown on a nonstick griddle.**

Efficiency Tip: Instead of grinding nuts and chopping the onion, place water and all ingredients (except oats and bulgur wheat) in a blender. Cover and turn on for 2 or 3 seconds, just long enough for all to go through the blades and get chopped fine, but not pureed. Then proceed as in step 1.

You can adjust the seasonings in this according to your taste. Try adding 1 tablespoon each molasses and tomato puree for a richer flavor. Make a chili burger by replacing the Italian seasoning with 1 teaspoon cumin and 1 tablespoon California Chili, or ½ package of mild taco seasoning. Just be sure to get plenty of flavor in your burger! Remember, it is usually eaten in a bun with burger fixings, and if the burger is bland, you will hardly know it's there.

REPLACEMENTS FOR BURGER

An easy way to replace hamburger in recipes is to use canned vegetarian alternatives such as Loma Linda Vegeburger, or a dried product often referred to as textured vegetable protein (TVP) made from soy. These products are good to have on hand for occasional use, and they can be a great boost for beginning vegetarian cooks. We have two recipes that provide a better choice—Bulgur Burger (below) and Veggie Cutlets (ground) (p. 37). They're not hard to make, they taste good, and they can be frozen and ready to use for quick entrées such as Hardy Hash (p. 111) or Shepherd's Pie (p. 38). (They'll save you money, too!)

BULGUR BURGER

1 cup bulgur wheat

1¼ cups water

½ cup walnuts, ground

1 tablespoons dried onion flakes

1 clove garlic (or ½ teaspoon powder)

1 tablespoon food yeast flakes

½ teaspoon salt

1 tablespoon Bragg Liquid Aminos (or increase salt to 1 teaspoon)

1 tablespoon Beef-Like Seasoning

8-ounce can tomato sauce

1. **Mix all ingredients together in a saucepan and bring to a boil. Reduce heat, cover, and simmer until thick. Remove from heat and let sit covered for 10 minutes.**

2. **Use as is, or place in a Teflon skillet over medium-high heat and brown, stirring now and then. If desired, add about 1 cup diced onion and brown with the bulgur wheat.**

Variation: *Bulgur Taco Filling* Replace *Beef-Like Seasoning* with ½ package mild taco seasoning or 1 tablespoon *Homemade Taco Seasoning* (p. 46). Serve in tacos, burritos, or tostadas.

Makes 3 cups.

"A causal relationship between red meat consumption and cancer is supported by several large studies conducted in the U.S. Specifically, women with the highest level of meat consumption had double the rate of breast cancer compared to those who consumed small amounts of meat."

Epidemiology 5, no. 4 (1994): 391

"The beef industry has contributed to more American deaths than all the wars of this century, all natural disasters, and all automobile accidents combined. If beef is your idea of real food for real people, you'd better live real close to a real good hospital."

Neal Barnard, M.D., Physicians Committee for Responsible Medicine

"Cancers, tumors, and various other inflammatory diseases are largely caused by meat eating. From the light which God has given me, the prevalence of cancers and tumors is largely due to gross living on dead flesh."

E. G. White, Healthful Living, pp. 100, 101

Veggie Cutlets

Bread Dressing

BREAD DRESSING

3 stalks celery, chopped fine

1 cup chopped onion

1 tablespoon Bragg Liquid Aminos

1½ tablespoons Chicken-Like Seasoning

½ teaspoon Italian seasoning

1 teaspoon sage

1 tablespoon parsley flakes

½ teaspoon garlic powder

2 cups water

9 cups toasted whole wheat Croutons (below)

1. Simmer celery, onion, and seasonings in the water until tender.

2. Place cubed bread in a large mixing bowl and toss with the simmered onions and seasonings. If water is not sufficient to moisten the bread cubes, sprinkle enough water over the mix to do so, but don't make it mushy. Cubes should not lose their shape.

3. Place in one large or two small bread pans that have been coated with a light nonstick spray. Cover with foil and place in a pan of water in a 400°F oven for 1 hour. Check in 30 minutes and, if it seems a bit dry, sprinkle with water.

Serving Tip: Good served with gravy. Place on a platter surrounded by baked potatoes or overlapped slices of Veggie Cutlets (p. 37). Delicious as a stuffing for butternut, acorn, or sweet meat squash.

❧*Makes 8 servings.*

Stove Top Variation: Instead of baking, you can place the dressing in a nonstick skillet over medium-low heat. Cover and let it cook for about 10 minutes. Remove lid and stir, then cover and let it brown on the bottom. Stir again and serve. This is a simple way to reheat leftover baked Bread Dressing.

CROUTONS

One large loaf of whole wheat bread will usually make 9 cups toasted cubes. Stack four slices at a time on a cutting board and slice into 1-inch cubes. Pour the cubes onto a large baking sheet and bake in the oven at 300°F for about 45 minutes or until dry. For salad croutons, toss in 1 teaspoon garlic salt before baking.

eplacing meat in recipes: Do you wish you could still make those tempting recipes with chicken, turkey, scallops, or beef? Don't throw those cookbooks away—you can replace! If you don't want to rely on canned or frozen vegetarian meat analogs, try making your own delicious and nutritious replacements free of refined fats.

VEGGIE CUTLETS

Here's a meaty chicken- or turkeylike substitute. It freezes beautifully, and is low in cost—a little goes a long way. We first learned about this recipe from Lance, one of our chefs at Five Loaves. He made it for our Thanksgiving buffet, and it became a favorite that we included in our Best Gourmet Recipes *cookbook. We learned later that the original recipe is "Mock Chicken" in Gloria Lawson's cookbook,* Tasty Vegan Delights. *Here's our adaptation.*

2 cups soaked soybeans or garbanzos (if you use canned garbanzos: drain the liquid into a measuring cup and add water to equal 1½ cups total liquid)

2 tablespoons soy sauce or ¼ cup Bragg Liquid Aminos

3 tablespoons Chicken-Like Seasoning

2 tablespoons yeast flakes

1 tablespoon onion powder

½ teaspoon garlic powder

2 cups gluten flour

1. **To soak soybeans or garbanzos, place at least 1 cup dry beans in about 2 cups of water and leave at room temperature for about 12 hours.**

2. **Place 2 cups of soaked, drained beans in a blender with 1½ cups water and blend.**

3. **While blending, add seasonings and blend smooth.**

4. **Pour into a bowl and add the gluten flour. It will become very stiff, and the last of the flour should be kneaded in with your hands. Knead for 2 minutes. If it is too soft (not holding together in an elastic ball), knead in ¼- ½ cup more gluten flour. This can be done in an electric bread mixer or by hand. Longer kneading will make a final product that is more chewy and elastic, while less kneading will make a final product that is more spongy and breadlike.**

5. **Form into two oval-shaped loaves and place on an oiled cookie sheet. Bake 50 minutes at 350°F. Cool on a rack. May be frozen.**

6. **When cool, slice very thin (about ⅛ inch) and simmer in the following broth for 5 minutes:**

BROTH

4 cups water

2 tablespoons Bragg Liquid Aminos

2 tablespoons Chicken-Like or Beef-Like Seasoning (depending on flavor desired)

7. **For a slightly thicker broth (which makes a richer, more attractive presentation), dissolve 1½ tablespoons cornstarch in ¼ cup water and gradually stir into the simmering cutlets.**

8. **Serve with mashed potatoes or Bread Dressing (p. 36) or make into Creamy Stroganoff (p. 29).**

Variation: *Cutlet Burger*
Cut one Veggie Cutlet loaf into several pieces. Place in food processor and blend briefly with steel blade to obtain the texture of ground round burger.

Use in recipes calling for burger, such as Shepherd's Pie (p. 38).

🍃*Makes 2 veggie cutlet loaves. Keep in freezer.*

CHICK STEW

One of the best ready-made meatlike products we have found is Soy Curls. They are made from soybeans that have been cooked, mashed, extruded, and dried—and that's all. Nothing added or removed. When soaked or simmered in seasoned water for a few minutes, they absorb the flavor you give them and have a chewy texture resembling chicken or beef. Good in fajitas, stir-fries, or stews.

1 cup Soy Curls

½ large onion, diced

3 cloves garlic, pressed

½ teaspoon salt

1 cup water

1½ cup diced potato

½ cup water or juice from tomatoes

½ teaspoon salt

1 teaspoon cumin

½ tablespoon California Chili

2 teaspoon onion powder

1 tablespoon Bragg Liquid Aminos or 2 teaspoons soy sauce

2 cups sliced zucchini or cut green beans

1 cup frozen corn

14-ounce can diced tomatoes, drained (or 2 cups fresh diced tomatoes)

1. **Place Soy Curls, diced onion, garlic, salt, and water in a kettle or nonstick skillet, and simmer until water is evaporated.**

2. **Add potatoes and ½ cup more water with ½ teaspoon salt and remaining seasonings. Simmer 8 minutes.**

3. **Add zucchini and cook 5 more minutes, then add corn and tomatoes. Heat and serve. Salt to taste.**

Variation: *Instead of Soy Curls, use 2 cups cooked black, red, or kidney beans, drained, adding them in step 3. Reduce water to ¼ cup in step 1.*

🍃*Makes 6 servings.*

Shepherd's Pie

We're not sure where the name came from for this time-honored favorite—perhaps from the simple "piecrust" topping made from mashed potatoes. This is another good example of how meat replacements can be used in traditional recipes.

4 cups diced raw potatoes

4 cups green beans (or 1 cup each: onions, sliced carrots, cabbage, and green beans)

1 cup water

1 teaspoon Italian seasoning

2 teaspoons Beef-Like Seasoning

1½ teaspoons onion powder

1 teaspoon salt

½ teaspoon garlic powder

1 cup burger substitute (p. 35)

2 cans tomato soup (option: instead of tomato soup, blend ½ can coconut milk with a 14-ounce can [1½ cups] of tomatoes)

1 cup coconut, cashew, or soy milk

½ teaspoon salt

water as needed

1. Place potatoes in saucepan, cover with water, and simmer 20 minutes or until soft.

2. Meanwhile, place green beans or vegetables in a saucepan with the seasonings and about 1 cup water (enough to almost cover the vegetables). Bring to a boil, then simmer for about 10 minutes. Add burger and simmer 10 more minutes.

3. Add the tomato soup and stir for 1 or 2 minutes while heating the whole mixture almost to boiling. Place in a

deep 1½-quart or 9" x 9" casserole dish.

4. Drain the potatoes and mash with milk and salt. Spread mashed potatoes over the top, forming a 1-inch layer or crust.

The potatoes are much easier to spread over the vegetable filling if they are freshly mashed, but leftover mashed potatoes may be used if heated and beaten with a little water or milk to make them spreadable. Or, instead of covering the top evenly, scoop or shape with your hands biscuit-sized potato mounds over the top and broil.

5. Place on a low shelf in the oven with broiler on for 5-10 minutes. Serve.

Tip: May be made ahead and refrigerated. Place uncovered in oven, and bake at 400°F for about 20 minutes until hot.

❧*Makes 6 servings.*

RATATOUILLE STIR-FRY WITH TOFU

1 medium onion, diced

1 green or red bell pepper

2 cloves garlic, crushed

1 tablespoon Bragg Liquid Aminos

1 teaspoon onion powder

1 tablespoon Chicken-Like Seasoning

1 teaspoon basil

2 small yellow summer squash or green zucchini, sliced

2 roma tomatoes, diced

1 recipe Marinated Baked Tofu (p. 39)

1. Place onions and green or red pepper in skillet along with garlic and seasonings. Add about ¼ cup water and cover. Simmer for 1 minute.

2. Add the sliced zucchini or yellow squash and diced tomatoes and sprinkle with ½ teaspoon salt. Add a small amount of water (enough to keep from sticking, but not more than can be absorbed in about 4 more minutes of cooking). Cover and simmer for about 2 minutes. Uncover and gently stir, cooking until vegetables are just beginning to become tender (don't overcook). Stir in Marinated Baked Tofu.

✺*Makes 5 cups.*

Variation: *Sweet and Sour Vegetables Replace diced roma tomatoes with a 15-ounce can petite diced tomatoes, one 8-ounce can crushed pineapple, ½ cup coconut milk, and 1 tablespoon cornstarch dissolved in ¼ cup water. Stir and heat to thicken. Serve over rice.*

✺*Makes 8 cups.*

MARINATED BAKED TOFU

Keep tofu on hand. It can be sliced or diced, flavored and baked to be used in sandwiches or tossed into stir-fries, curries, or stews in the place of chicken.

½ brick firm tofu (8 ounces)

1 tablespoon soy sauce or Bragg Liquid Aminos

1½ teaspoons Chicken-Like Seasoning

Dice tofu and place in a bowl with soy sauce and Chicken-Like Seasoning; gently stir to coat. Fry on medium-high heat in a nonstick skillet, turning occasionally until browned. Or bake on a cookie sheet (line with Bake Magic) at 400°F until golden brown and puffy.

BARBECUE TOFU

A flavor-filled dish that makes a delicious entrée. Serve with rice or mashed potatoes. The delicately sweet sauce becomes creamy with the addition of peanut butter or dry-roasted peanuts.

16-ounce package extra-firm tofu
   (freeze overnight for more chewy texture)

¾ cup water

2 tablespoons Bragg Liquid Aminos

2 tablespoons honey or more to taste

¾ teaspoon salt or butter-flavored salt

½ teaspoon garlic powder

1 teaspoon Wright's Hickory Seasoning (optional)

1 teaspoon paprika

15-ounce can petite diced tomatoes in juice

2 tablespoons peanut butter or ¼ cup dry-roasted peanuts

1 teaspoon onion powder

2 tablespoons dried onion flakes (or 1 small onion, diced and steamed in some of the seasoning sauce)

1 tablespoon dried parsley flakes

1. Cut the tofu in ½-inch slices or dice in 1-inch cubes.

2. Combine water, Bragg's, honey, salt, garlic powder, Hickory Seasoning, and paprika in a saucepan. Add the tofu slices or cubes. Bring to a boil, reduce heat, and simmer, covered, for 10 minutes.

3. Drain off the water into blender container, and gently place the tofu on an oiled or Bake Magic-lined cookie sheet. Place on bottom rack of oven. Bake at 400°F for about 20 minutes, turning after 10 minutes. Or brown on both sides in a nonstick skillet.

Tip: At this point, tofu is delicious as is or used in sandwiches.

4. Meanwhile, drain the juice from the diced tomatoes into the blender along with the liquid from simmering the tofu. Add remaining ingredients (except the diced tomatoes, onions, and parsley) and blend smooth.

5. Placed baked tofu in a 9-inch square baking dish, overlapping slightly. Combine blended sauce with diced tomatoes, onion, and parsley flakes. Pour over the tofu and bake at 400°F for 30 minutes.

✺*Makes 4-6 servings.*

"Persons who have accustomed themselves to a rich, highly stimulating diet have an unnatural taste, and they cannot at once relish food that is plain and simple. It will take time for the taste to become natural and for the stomach to recover from the abuse it has suffered. But those who persevere in the use of wholesome food will, after a time, find it palatable. Its delicate and delicious flavors will be appreciated, and it will be eaten with greater enjoyment than can be derived from unwholesome dainties. And the stomach, in a healthy condition, neither fevered nor overtaxed, can readily perform its task."

E. G. White, The Ministry of Healing, *pp. 298, 299*

"Evidence strongly suggests that a high intake of plant-based foods and a low intake of animal products contributes to the excellent health of Mediterranean populations. The high consumption of red meat in Western diets is associated with increased risks of heart disease, some cancers, and urinary calcium losses likely to contribute to osteoporosis."

American Journal of Clinical Nutrition *61 (1995): 1416*

"A variety of simple dishes, perfectly healthful and nourishing, may be provided, aside from meat. Hearty men must have plenty of vegetables, fruits, and grains."

E. G. White, Counsels on Diet and Foods, *p. 407*

Sweet Tomato Topping

Holiday Nut Loaf

Hint: A food processor will greatly simplify the preparation of this loaf. The bread can easily be made into crumbs several slices at a time, the nuts can be ground, and the onions chopped. These bread crumbs are made using soft, untoasted bread. Dried crumbs are more compact, so if you use them, use only 1½-2 cups.

3. Place mix in lightly oiled or nonstick loaf pan. Cover with foil and bake at 350°F for 1 hour. Remove foil and bake uncovered for 30 minutes. Remove from oven and let cool for about 5 minutes to give it a chance to set up before removing from the pan. Turn upside down onto a serving dish. Garnish with fresh parsley or kale and serve with Simple Gravy (p. 76) or Sweet and Sour Tomato Sauce (p. 41).

Variation: *Cashew-Carrot Loaf Follow Holiday Nut Loaf recipe using 2 cups raw cashew nuts in place of the pecans. Use 1 cup finely ground or grated carrot and reduce onion to 1 cup finely chopped onion. Use 1 tablespoon Chicken-Like Seasoning in place of the Bragg Liquid Aminos.*

Serving Tips: A good entrée for a holiday meal along with cranberries, mashed potatoes, and gravy.

This loaf freezes well.

Leftover loaf is delicious when slices are placed in a nonstick skillet and browned on each side. Yummy in sandwiches or burgers.

☙*Makes 1 loaf (10 servings).*

SWEET TOMATO TOPPING

8-ounce can crushed pineapple

8-ounce can tomato sauce

1 tablespoon molasses

½ teaspoon basil

¼ teaspoon garlic powder

Use the five ingredients above or simply:

2 cups mild salsa and 1 cup purchased sugarless grape jam

Combine in a small bowl and serve over Holiday Nut Loaf (p. 40) or Tofu-Walnut Balls (p. 41).

☙*Makes 2 cups.*

HOLIDAY NUT LOAF

No vegetarian cookbook would be complete without a good savory meatloaf. Here's a tried-and-true recipe that you will love. It is a basic recipe that lends itself well to variations. If you live in areas of the world where pecans are rare, use your local nuts.

If you don't have tofu, use soybeans. Seasonings can be varied too, according to what you like. This recipe includes a large amount of onions. At first I thought that sounded like too much, but now I consider it to be the secret of its wonderful flavor and moist texture. The tofu or soybeans and gluten flour or cornstarch help bind it together, replacing the eggs.

1 cup tofu and ½ cup water (or 1 cup soaked soybeans with 1 cup water)

2 cloves garlic, minced (or 1 teaspoon garlic powder)

1 tablespoon **Bragg Liquid Aminos** or 2 teaspoons soy sauce

¼ cup gluten flour or cornstarch

1½ teaspoons salt

1 tablespoon onion powder

1 teaspoon ground sage or Italian seasoning

3-4 cups soft whole grain bread crumbs

2 cups pecans (may use walnuts, almonds, peanuts, sunflower seeds, or cashews)

2 cups finely chopped onions

1. Blend tofu (or soybeans) with water, garlic, and seasonings.

2. Combine remaining ingredients in a mixing bowl. Add blended tofu or soybeans and mix well.

Sweet and Sour Meatballs Over Rice

1 recipe Tofu-Walnut Balls (p. 41)

1 recipe Sweet and Sour Tomato Sauce (p. 41)

1 recipe Fluffy Brown Rice (p. 49)

Place baked balls in a serving dish and pour hot Sweet and Sour Tomato Sauce over them. Serve with Fluffy Brown Rice.

Tofu-Walnut Balls

2 cups soft bread crumbs

¾ cup finely chopped walnuts

½ cup quick oats

½ cup finely diced onions (or ¼ cup dried onion flakes)

½ teaspoon garlic powder

1 teaspoon onion powder

½ teaspoon Vege-Sal

1 teaspoon Italian seasoning

2 teaspoons Chicken-Like Seasoning

16-ounce brick tofu

½ cup water

2 tablespoons Bragg Liquid Aminos

1. Place bread crumbs, walnuts, oats, onions, and seasonings in a large mixing bowl.

Hint: Make bread crumbs out of slices of bread in your blender or food processor. Next whiz the walnuts into fine pieces about the size of coarse meal. If using a food processor, the onion can be finely chopped too.

2. Blend tofu with water and Liquid Aminos in blender; add to the bread crumb mixture in the bowl and mix well.

3. Place in mounds on a nonstick or oiled cookie sheet. If desired, flatten balls into small patties. Bake at 350°F for 30 minutes or until golden brown on top and bottom.

Hint: The easiest way to make these is with an ice-cream scoop (large, medium, or small—whatever size you like). The mix should be quite moist—too wet to make balls with your hands. The dryness of your bread-crumbs will make a difference—add more water if they seem too dry. A dry mix makes a heavier, drier product, whereas a moist mix results in a lighter, more moist, and superior product.

4. Serve with Sweet and Sour Tomato Sauce (p. 41) or pasta sauce.

Hint: Keep a bagful of these "meatballs" in your freezer, and you will find endless uses for them.

Sweet and Sour Tomato Sauce

3 cups pineapple juice

14-ounce can diced tomatoes or stewed tomatoes

½ cup tomato paste or puree

1-2 tablespoons honey (optional)

1 onion, cut in fourths

1 green pepper, cut in fourths

3 cloves garlic, minced

1 teaspoon basil

1 tablespoon salt (or less to taste)

1 tablespoon onion powder

3 tablespoons cornstarch

1. Place all ingredients in blender and blend for a few seconds, just enough to chop the onion and pepper, but not puree.

2. Pour into a saucepan and bring to a boil; reduce heat and simmer for about 10 minutes.

3. Mix about 3 tablespoons cornstarch in a small amount of water and slowly stir into the simmering sauce until it is as thick as you like it.

Sweet and Sour Tomato Sauce

Tofu-Walnut Balls

Beans and Rice

Tostadas

Fajitas

Nothing can equal the easy availability of the Mexican tortilla—not to mention its low cost. What a contribution to our way of eating it has become! But can it be prepared healthfully without frying in lots of oil? The recipes in this section will really improve the quality of your Mexican fare.

CRISPY TORTILLAS FOR TOSTADAS

Webster's definition of a tostada is "a tortilla fried in deep fat." But frying in fat results in many health problems. Here is how to make the tortilla crispy without frying.

1 dozen corn tortillas

2 wire cooling racks

1. Preheat oven to 400°F.

2. Place tortillas on a wire cooling rack with a second rack on top (upside down with legs up; the tortillas are pressed flat between the two racks).

3. Place racks with tortillas between in preheated oven. Bake about 10 minutes, watching carefully so they don't burn. They may need 11-12 minutes and should be light brown—not too brown and not too light. If undercooked, they will be tough. If left too long, they will taste burned. Experience will help you get them just right—golden brown and tender!

SOFT CORN TORTILLAS

This method of cooking tortillas replaces the traditional way of frying them in oil, but still gives enough strength so that they are less likely to tear or break open when rolled.

1. Preheat a nonstick or well-seasoned cast-iron skillet to medium-hot.

2. Meanwhile, place about 1 cup water in a shallow bowl or pie plate and add ½ teaspoon salt if desired.

3. Dip tortillas in the water, one at a time, and place on the hot skillet, 30 seconds on each side. Or place one at a time in microwave 40-50 seconds.

4. Stack between towels and continue to cook as many tortillas as needed.

TOSTADAS OR SOFT TACOS

Tostadas made with crispy corn tortillas or tacos made with soft corn tortillas are always a favorite.

12 tostada shells or soft corn tortillas

2 cups mashed pinto or black beans, heated

2 cups **Bulgur Taco Filling** (p. 35) or **Fiesta Salad** rice mixture (p. 44), heated

1 cup **Fresh Picadillo** (p. 49)

1 cup diced avocados or **Avocado Guacamole** (p. 47)

shredded **Sliceable Cashew Cheese** (p. 73) or **Chedda Polenta** (p. 66)

diced tomatoes and shredded lettuce

Spread each tostada shell or warm soft tortilla with a layer of mashed beans, **Bulgur Burger** (taco filling variation) (p. 35), or **Fiesta Rice** (p. 44). Then drizzle with salsa, and add guacamole, diced tomatoes, and shredded lettuce. Try not to load it up too much, so the tostada or soft taco can be eaten with the hand. Good served with fruit smoothies and baked tortilla chips with fresh salsa or guacamole for dip.

Serves 4.

CRISPY BAKED TORTILLA CHIPS

Picture on page 58.

1 cup water

1 teaspoon salt

1 package whole wheat tortillas

garlic powder

onion powder

1. Pour water into a mixing bowl, add salt, and stir to dissolve. Dip each tortilla in the salted water.

2. Stack three or four tortillas on a cutting board, and cut through all layers with a sharp knife like a pie, making eight triangles out of each tortilla.

3. Arrange cut tortillas on cookie sheets; close together, but not overlapping. Sprinkle with garlic and onion powder, or other seasonings of choice.

4. Bake in oven at 350°F for 10 minutes or until crisp and beginning to brown slightly. Serve with salsa or **Creamy Chipotle Pepper Dressing** (p. 58)

CRISPY BAKED PITA CHIPS

Split uncut pita bread into two circles and cut into six or eight pie-shaped triangles or into strips. Arrange on a cookie sheet and bake at 350°F for 15-20 minutes, or at 175°F overnight. Serve with **Humus Tahini** (p. 58) or **Avocado Dip** (p. 69).

"A high-fat, animal-based diet is the single most significant cause of death from heart disease."

Roger R. Williams, in Nutrition in the '90's, *pp. 237-316*

"Many who adopt the health reform complain that it does not agree with them; but after sitting at their tables I come to the conclusion that it is not the health reform that is at fault, but the poorly prepared food. I appeal to men and women to whom God has given intelligence: learn how to cook. I make no mistake when I say men, for they, as well as women, need to understand the simple, healthful preparation of food."

E. G. White, Counsels on Health, *p. 155*

Creamy Chipotle Dressing

Fiesta Salad

FIESTA SALAD

1 recipe **Fluffy Brown Rice** (p. 49)

1 cup burger replacement (p. 35)

1 onion, diced

1 red, yellow, or orange pepper

½ teaspoon cumin

½ teaspoon **California Chili**

½ teaspoon garlic powder or 1 clove fresh garlic, pressed

8 cups chopped Romaine lettuce

2 tomatoes, diced

1 large or 2 small avocados

Creamy Chipotle Pepper Dressing (p. 58)

1 cup shredded **Sliceable Cashew Cheese** (p. 73), **Chedda Polenta** (p. 66), or equivalent from store

1. Sauté onion, pepper, and seasonings together in ½ cup water for 5 minutes, or until water is evaporated.

2. Add burger and rice. Fry for 2 more minutes, stirring occasionally.

3. Divide lettuce onto four dinner plates. Top with hot rice-burger mixture, chipotle dressing, and diced tomatoes, avocados, and shredded cheese. Serve.

Serves 4.

TAMALES

Traditionally tamales are made with plenty of oil in the masa *(dough). This is a favorite of our grandchildren, who often request them for birthday parties. In place of the oil we tried coconut milk, and the result was a wonderful soft and moist dough sure to please any tamale lover!*

half 8-ounce package dried corn husks

2 cups **Masa Harina Flour**

1 can coconut milk

2 tablespoons water, or more as needed

1 teaspoon salt

½ tablespoon **Chicken-Like Seasoning**

Tamale Filling:

1 cup burger replacement (p. 35)

2 tablespoons dried onion flakes

1 teaspoon **Homemade Taco Seasoning** (p. 46)

¼ cup water, or more to moisten

Simmer together until moisture is evaporated, then add 2 tablespoons Simple Mayonnaise (p. 57).

1. Soak dried corn husks several hours (place in a bowl or bread pan and cover with water). Use a weight on top to keep them submerged.

2. Combine in a mixing bowl *masa* flour and seasonings. Stir in coconut milk and water to form a soft dough. Divide into 12 balls.

The dough should be soft, but not sticking to hands. Press some of it into a flat pancake in your hand; if it cracks and doesn't hold together, add a bit more water.

3. Place corn husks, one at a time, on a flat surface or plate. With your fingers, flatten dough on each husk ¼ inch thick, leaving about a 1-inch margin at the bottom and sides. Place 1-2 tablespoons Tamale Filling (p. 44) lengthwise down the center. Lift long husk sides toward the center, gently sliding the dough away from the husk to cover the filling. Overlap and press edges of dough together, forming a tube of *masa* filled with burger.

4. Fold the narrow end of the husk up and the sides in—forming a long corn-husk covering for the tamale.

5. Place tamales in a steamer basket in a kettle over boiling water. Cover and steam for 1 hour.

6. Serve hot in husks (each one removes the husk to eat the tamale.) Good with salsa or guacamole. May be frozen.

Tip: Oven reheating makes tamale dry; it's best to reheat in a steamer or microwave.

Makes 12.

FAJITAS

See page 42 for a picture of this simple Mexican meal. Usually roasted vegetables, beans, or chicken are served with warmed, soft corn or flour tortillas. Extras to add include shredded lettuce, picadillo or salsa, and cheese or guacamole. Here are three different fillings that easily replace the meat in this meal and are also good in Santa Fe Burritos (p. 47) or Vegetable Wraps (p. 75).

PORTABELLA MUSHROOM FILLING

1 large onion, diced

1-2 cloves garlic, pressed

½ teaspoon Italian seasoning

2 tablespoons Bragg Liquid Aminos

2 large portabella mushrooms

2 teaspoons lime juice (optional)

½ teaspoon salt (or more), to taste

1. Place onion, garlic, , and seasonings in nonstick or cast-iron skillet. Add ½ cup water and simmer until water is evaporated. Continue cooking the onion until it browns a bit, and add 1 tablespoon more water. See how to "caramelize" an onion on page 50 (sidebar).

2. Slice mushrooms in ¼-inch slices as you would a loaf of bread; then cut across slices in thirds.

3. Add mushrooms and remaining ingredients to caramelized onion and cover. As mushrooms cook they will make enough liquid to steam with the onion. Simmer uncovered for 10 minutes until most of the juice is evaporated. Serve in Fajitas (above).

Makes 4-5 cups.

ROASTED VEGETABLE FILLING

½ cup Soy Curls or 8 ounces firm tofu, cut into ½-inch cubes

⅓ cup water

1 teaspoon Chicken-Like Seasoning

1 teaspoon yeast flakes

1 tablespoon Bragg Liquid Aminos

1 medium bell pepper, diced

1 medium red onion, cut into ½-inch wedges

1 medium zucchini, cut lengthwise and then into ¼-inch slices

1 cup broccoli, cut into small pieces (optional)

¼ pound fresh mushrooms, cut into fourths (optional)

Sweet and Sour Marinade: Combine 1 tablespoon Bragg Liquid Aminos with 1 tablespoon honey, 1 teaspoon lemon juice, and ½ teaspoon salt.

1. Combine Soy Curls with water and seasonings in a small saucepan or microwave container. Bring to a boil and let stand 10 minutes. If using tofu, omit water and coat with same seasonings.

2. Set oven to broil. Combine vegetables with Sweet and Sour Marinade (p. 52) in a bowl and mix to coat vegetables. Drain off excess. Add soaked Soy Curls or seasoned tofu. Spread mixture on lightly greased cookie sheet. Broil uncovered 5 to 10 minutes or until crisp-tender.

3. Serve in Fajitas (above) or Vegetable Wraps (p. 75), or as a filling for Santa Fe Burritos (p. 47).

Makes 4 cups, fills 10 wraps.

TEX-MEX FILLING

1 onion, diced

¼ cup water

1 teaspoon Chicken-Like Seasoning

¼ teaspoon salt

2 cloves garlic, minced

2 cups cooked rice (salted when cooked)

1 cup each: frozen corn, cooked black beans, burger replacement (p. 35)

1-2 cups fresh diced tomatoes

2 teaspoons cumin

1 teaspoon California Chili

2-3 tablespoons chopped fresh cilantro

1. Place diced onion in nonstick skillet over medium-high heat with water, Chicken-Like Seasoning, and salt. Cook until caramelized (see p. 50).

2. Add remaining ingredients and heat to serving temperature.

3. Serve in soft tortillas or crisp tostada shells. Top with Avocado Guacamole (p. 47) or Tofu Sour Cream (p. 58) and shredded lettuce.

Makes 6 cups.

Black Bean
Enchiladas

Santa Fe
Burritos

VEGETABLE BLACK BEAN ENCHILADAS

12 corn tortillas

Filling:

3 cups finely chopped vegetables (onion, sweet bell peppers, green or yellow zucchini, mushrooms, and spinach may be used)

1 tablespoon **Bragg Liquid Aminos** or 1 teaspoon soy sauce

¼ teaspoon salt

¼ teaspoon garlic powder

¼ teaspoon cumin

¼ teaspoon basil

Topping:

1 can black beans, drained

1 cup fresh or frozen corn

¼ cup chopped sweet or green onion

¼ teaspoon cumin

¼ teaspoon salt

1 teaspoon lime juice (may use lemon)

15-ounce can seasoned petite diced tomatoes in juice, or 2 cups salsa or pasta sauce of choice

2 cups **Simple Cheese Sauce** (p. 26)

1-2 tablespoons chopped fresh cilantro leaves

1. **Preheat a nonstick or well-seasoned cast-iron skillet to medium-hot.**

2. **Meanwhile, place about 1 cup water in a shallow bowl or pie plate.**

3. **Dip tortillas in the water, one at a time, and place on the hot skillet, 30 seconds on each side.**

4. **Cover cooked tortillas with a towel—if they are warm and moist, they stay pliable for rolling into enchiladas.**

5. **Place filling vegetables and seasonings in the nonstick skillet, and add about 2 tablespoons water. Cover and cook on medium-high for 6-7 minutes. Lift lid and stir every 2 minutes.**

6. **Using an oblong casserole dish (Pyrex 9" x 13" or similar), cover the bottom with the canned petite diced tomatoes or salsa and ¾ cup of the Cheese Sauce. Place a small amount of filling in each tortilla and roll up. Place on top of the tomato sauce in** the casserole dish, and drizzle top with remaining Cheese Sauce.

7. **Mix together the topping and arrange down the center of the rolled tortillas. Garnish with fresh cilantro leaves and bake covered for 30 minutes at 350°F until heated through. Remove cover during last five minutes.**

Serves 4-6.

HOMEMADE TACO SEASONING

2 tablespoons onion powder

3 tablespoons paprika

2 tablespoons salt

1 tablespoon garlic powder

¼ cup cumin

¼ cup **California Chili**

Mix together and store in an airtight container.

Makes ½ cup.

SANTA FE BURRITOS

Thanks to Rilla Klingbeil for this idea. You can use white four tortillas, but the whole wheat tortillas are softened by the sauce when heated, and your family will hardly know the difference.

- 8-10 large whole wheat flour tortillas
- 8-ounce can tomato sauce
- 2 14-ounce cans Mexican stewed tomatoes, blend briefly or mash
- 2 cups cooked, mashed pinto or black beans (or canned vegetarian no-oil, refried beans)*
- 2 cups Simple Cheese Sauce (p. 26)

1. Lightly coat an oblong baking dish (about 9" x 13") with cooking spray or oil, and cover the bottom with half the tomato sauce and one can mashed Mexican stewed tomatoes.

2. Thinly spread entire surface of each tortilla with mashed beans and roll up.

3. Nestle each rolled tortilla into the tomato sauce in the casserole dish, one layer deep.

Hint: I like to cut them in half if they are a large flour tortilla—easier to serve!

4. Spread Simple Cheese Sauce over the burritos—then spread the other can of tomato sauce and Mexican stewed tomatoes over the top, using a spoon or rubber spatula to let some of the Cheese Sauce show through the tomatoes. Garnish with fresh cilantro leaves and sliced black olives if desired.

5. Bake at 350°F about 30 minutes and serve.

*Variation: *Use Roasted Vegetable Filling (p. 45) in burritos instead of beans.*

❧*Serves 6-8.*

QUICK SKILLET BURRITOS

Place sauce, rolled burritos, and cheese in a nonstick electric skillet (use same order given above for a casserole), cover and heat on medium temperature until hot.

Tip: Individual servings of this recipe can be made using the amount of tortillas desired with cheese and seasoned tomato sauce, and heating in a small skillet on the stove or small casserole in the microwave.

SIMPLE ENCHILADAS

Follow the Santa Fe Burrito recipe, but use corn tortillas instead of flour tortillas. Prepare the corn tortillas by dipping in water and heating on a skillet (see Soft Corn Tortillas [p. 43]).

STACKED ENCHILADA BAKE

This casserole is a perfect last-minute dish. Shredded lettuce, chopped tomatoes, and Tofu Sour Cream (p. 58) or guacamole make tasty "fixins" to top each serving.

- 12 corn tortillas, torn into bite-size pieces*
- 4 cups seasoned black beans or chili
- 14-ounce can Mexican-style tomatoes (blend briefly or mash)
- 1½ cups Simple Cheese Sauce (p. 26)
- 3 medium green onions, sliced (¼ cup)
- 1 cup sliced black olives

1. Heat oven to 400°F. Grease 2-quart casserole.

2. Place half the tortilla pieces in casserole and top with half the beans. Repeat layers. Pour 1 cup of the Cheese Sauce over the beans and tortilla pieces and then the canned tomatoes. Dot the top with the remaining Cheese Sauce and sprinkle with chopped onions and sliced olives.

3. Bake uncovered about 20 minutes or until bubbly around edge.

*Variation: *May use baked corn chips instead of corn tortillas (or regular corn chips, but the baked variety now available in stores have much less oil).*

❧*Serves 6-8.*

AVOCADO GUACAMOLE

- 1 ripe avocado
- 1 teaspoon lemon juice
- 2 or 3 tablespoons Tofu Sour Cream (p. 58) or Simple Mayonnaise (p. 57)
- ¼ teaspoon garlic powder
- salt to taste

Mash avocado and stir in remaining ingredients. Garnish with a cilantro leaf or red bell pepper. Serve with tortilla chips, burritos, or tamales, or on rye bread or Rye Krisp.

Dietary intake and the risk of coronary heart disease among the coconut-consuming Minangkabau in west Sumatra, Indonesia. (This is one of several studies indicating that coconut or its milk are not atherogenic when eaten whole!)

"In many populations, high intakes of saturated fat are associated with elevated serum cholesterol concentrations and increased coronary heart disease (CHD) mortality. However, several studies report that . . . heart diseases are not common among populations who consume coconut, a source of saturated fat. A case-control study was conducted among the Minangkabau known to be high coconut consumers to examine the difference in food patterns and risk of coronary heart disease. . . . Subjects with CHD were identified . . . [from] five participating hospitals . . . in west Sumatra, Indonesia. A total of 93 [subjects with CHD] . . . and 189 . . . controls . . . were recruited. . . . Intakes of individual foods . . . over the preceding 12 months was obtained. . . . The case group had significantly higher intakes of meats, eggs, sugar, tea, coffee and fruits, but lower intakes of soy products, rice and cereals compared to the controls. *Coconut consumption as flesh or milk was not different between cases and controls.* The cases [sick people] had significantly higher intakes of protein and cholesterol, but lower intake of carbohydrate. . . . The consumption of total fat or saturated fat, including that from coconut, was not a predictor for CHD in this food culture. However, the intakes of animal foods, total protein, dietary cholesterol and less plant-derived carbohydrates were predictors of CHD."

Asia Pacific Journal of Clinical Nutrition 13, no. 4 (December 2004): 377-384.

Chili With Corn

LITE AND TENDER CORN BREAD

¾ cup cornmeal

¾ cup whole wheat flour

½ teaspoon salt

1½ tablespoons Ener-G Baking Powder (or 2 teaspoons regular)

½ cup coconut milk (may use ½ cup plus 2 tablespoons soy milk and omit water)

¼ cup applesauce

2 tablespoons honey

2 tablespoons water or as needed

1. Mix together in a mixing bowl: corn-meal, flour, salt, and baking powder.

2. Stir together the coconut or soy milk, applesauce, and honey in measuring cup. Add water as needed to make 1 full cup of mixture.

3. Combine wet and dry ingredients, stirring briskly until smooth. Pour into an 8" x 8" pan, or scoop into muffin tins. Bake at 375°F for 20-25 minutes.

☙*Makes 9 squares.*

CHILI WITH CORN

½ cup diced onion

½ green or red pepper (optional)

1-2 cloves fresh garlic, crushed, or ½ teaspoon garlic powder

1 teaspoon cumin

1½ teaspoons California Chili

2 teaspoon onion powder

½ teaspoon salt

2 cups cooked black or small red beans (may be canned)

1½ cups frozen or fresh corn

14-ounce can diced tomatoes in juice

2 tablespoons molasses

1. Put onion, peppers, and seasonings in a medium-sized kettle and add about ½ cup water. Simmer for about 8 minutes until onion is tender.

2. Add remaining ingredients, and heat to serving temperature. Top with Tofu Sour Cream (p. 58) if desired.

☙*Makes 6 cups.*

EGGPLANT CHILI

Follow Chili With Corn recipe (p. 48), but instead of corn, use 2 cups finely diced, peeled eggplant. Just simmer it in the water with the onion and sea-sonings, using a bit more salt to taste.

I like to use a nonstick skillet or kettle and let the water evaporate until onions and eggplant brown slightly. Add ¼ cup water and stir to mix. Let evaporate and brown again, then add 2 tablespoons more water and stir again, thus "caramelizing" them (see p. 50 [sidebar]).

Add remaining ingredients and heat to serving temperature.

CORN PONE

1 recipe Chili With Corn (p. 48) or Eggplant Chili (p. 48)

1 recipe Lite and Tender Corn Bread (p. 48)

1. Place hot chili in a deep casserole dish.

2. Make corn bread batter and gently place one spoonful at a time on top of the chili. Spread to cover the chili as much as possible.

3. Bake in oven at 400°F for 25 minutes, or until corn topping begins to brown.

☙*Serves 8-10.*

FLUFFY BROWN RICE

Rice is a staple food around the world, but most cultures have found a way to make white rice the preferred choice. Replacing white with brown rice is not hard to do—just hard for most people to get used to. Here are some secrets that will help you make a more painless transition:

- Make the changes gradually if you have family members that need convincing.

- Start by serving rice that is half white mixed with half brown.

- Use long grain brown rice instead of short for a nicer appearance.

- Cook no more than three cups of rice in a kettle. Larger amounts of rice (2 to 3 cups) do better in a wide kettle. Cooked rice at the bottom of a deep, narrow kettle will be gummy.

- Follow this simple recipe when making brown rice, to keep it fluffy and not sticky and mushy:

2 cups water

1 cup rice

1 teaspoon salt

1. Bring water to a boil, then add salt and rice. Cover and cook on low heat for approximately 40 minutes. (If you live at an elevation of 4,000 feet or more, add ¼ cup more water and cook 10 minutes longer.)

2. When finished cooking, remove lid and fluff rice with a fork, or place in a shallow dish to let the steam escape so the rice doesn't get gummy on the bottom.

Makes 4 cups.

FRESH PICADILLO

1 cup finely diced fresh tomatoes
(or use canned tomatoes, drained)

4 sprigs fresh cilantro, chopped

¼ teaspoon garlic powder

½ teaspoon salt

1 teaspoon lime juice (optional)

Mix together and serve as a garnish or topping.

Makes 2 cups.

Variation: *Cucumber Picadillo (see picture on page 42). Add 1 cup finely diced cucumber.*

CUBAN BLACK BEANS

2½ cups dry black beans

5 cups water

½ cup diced green or red pepper

¼ cup diced dehydrated onions
(or 1 chopped fresh onion)

2 tablespoon yeast flakes

1½ teaspoons cumin

1½ teaspoons Chicken-Like Seasoning

1 teaspoon onion powder

¾ teaspoon garlic powder

¾ teaspoon sweet basil

2 tablespoons soy sauce

1 tablespoon lemon juice

1½ teaspoons Vege-Sal or
¾ teaspoon salt

1. Sort* black beans and soak in 10 cups water overnight, or bring to a boil, turn off heat, and let sit one hour.

Hint: To help reduce gastrointestinal distress, drain off water after the beans are finished soaking and add fresh water to 1 inch above the soaked beans.

2. Add remaining ingredients and bring to a boil, then simmer on low heat for about 1½ hours, or until tender. Serve over brown rice and garnish with Tofu Sour Cream (p. 58) and Cucumber Picadillo (p. 49) or Creamy Chipotle Pepper Dressing (p. 58).

Makes 8 cups.

*We find that pouring the beans onto a cookie pan allows us to pick out little bits of dirt, tiny stones, etc.

"Cow's milk has become a point of controversy among doctors and nutritionists. There was a time when it was considered very desirable, but research has forced us to rethink this recommendation. . . . Dairy products contribute to a surprising number of health problems."

Benjamin Spock, M.D., Dr. Spock's Baby and Child Care, *seventh edition*

"Dietary fat during childhood may be more life-threatening than was originally suspected. . . . Overweight children are usually the victims of the dietary habits of the adult members of the family. . . . Reducing dietary fats to levels necessary to the control of cholesterol cannot be achieved if a child drinks whole milk or eats cheese."

Charles Attwood, M.D., Dr. Attwood's Low-Fat Prescription for Kids

"As disease in animals increases, the use of milk and eggs will become more and more unsafe. An effort should be made to supply their place with other things that are healthful and inexpensive. The people everywhere should be taught how to cook without milk and eggs, so far as possible, and yet have their food wholesome and palatable."

E. G. White, Counsels on Diet and Foods, *p. 365*

Most recipes using onions begin with "sauté onions in oil." Why? To enhance their flavor and to prevent the finished dish from having an unpleasant boiled onion taste. Here are some secrets to keep the good taste while eliminating the harmful effects of frying.

Sautéing Without Oil

1. Place ½ cup of water in a skillet, then add some of the seasonings that are used in the recipe, such as salt, Bragg Liquid Aminos, garlic, or onion powder.

2. Add the onions, cover and let simmer in the flavored water until they are tender (about 10 minutes).

3. Remove the lid and continue simmering until most of the water is evaporated. You will find that the rich flavor associated with sautéing has been retained. This technique can be used in any recipe that calls for sautéing onions or vegetables in oil.

Caramelized Onions

1. Place the diced or sliced onions in a nonstick skillet with ¼ cup water. Add a little salt and pressed garlic or garlic powder. Simmer until water is gone, and let the onions begin to brown lightly.

2. Add 1 or 2 tablespoons water and stir, mixing the browned area that has begun to stick to the pan into the water until it dissolves and coats the onions. When this is evaporated, let the onions begin to brown again, then add more water and stir again.

3. Repeat this process three or four times until the onions are tender and caramel-colored. Use as a topping on baked potatoes or pizza, or in quiche, omelets, or other dishes.

STIR-FRY ORIENTAL

This is a basic recipe. Use other vegetables to create your own variations!

¼ cup water

1-2 cloves garlic, crushed, or ½ teaspoon garlic powder

1 tablespoon **Bragg Liquid Aminos** or ½ teaspoon salt

2 teaspoons lemon juice

½ tablespoon honey

1 teaspoon onion powder

1 cup each: sliced onion and thin carrot sticks*

2 cups each: broccoli and snow peas or sugar snap peas, stringed*

½ tablespoon cornstarch dissolved in ¼ cup water

1 cup roasted whole cashews (optional)

½ cup **Veggie Cutlets** (p. 37), cut in strips (optional)

1. **Place the water, garlic, and seasonings in a saucepan and add the onions, carrots, and broccoli. Cover and bring to a boil; reduce heat and simmer for 5 minutes.**

2. **Add the peas, Veggie Cutlets, and cashews. Simmer and stir in dissolved cornstarch until thick. Add a bit more water if needed to make the cornstarch mixture look juicy and not too starchy. Serve hot over rice.**

Variations: *Try other vegetable combinations using this basic recipe, such as:*

carrots, onions, green beans, and cauliflower

broccoli, red and yellow peppers, and onions

asparagus, red peppers, onions, and toasted sesame seeds

*Or for a quick dish, use a 16-ounce package frozen stir-fry vegetables. Add ½ cup Veggie Cutlet strips or whole, roasted cashew nuts.

Serves 4-6.

SUGAR PEAS AND CARROTS IN LIME SAUCE

This beautiful combination is bursting with flavor and eye appeal. See picture with Veggie Cutlets on page 36.

Follow Stir-fry Oriental (p. 50) recipe, replacing broccoli, peas, and onion with:

2 cups carrots

4 cups sugar snap peas (may use green beans or snow peas)

2 teaspoons lime juice instead of lemon

Serves 4-6.

ITALIAN GREEN BEANS WITH GARLIC AND TOMATOES

Green beans and red tomatoes, added after the beans are cooked to keep their bright red color, provide this dish with a double advantage—it looks good and it tastes good!

1 cup canned diced tomatoes in juice

1 cup finely chopped onion

2 cloves garlic, minced

¼ cup chopped fresh basil, or ½ teaspoon dried

1 teaspoon salt

14-ounce package frozen Italian flat green beans

1. **Drain the juice from the canned tomatoes into a large nonstick skillet, and cook onion, garlic, and seasonings in the juice for about 5 minutes.**

2. **Add green beans and ¼ cup water. Simmer until beans are tender, about 8 minutes. Remove from heat, stir in the tomatoes, and serve.**

Serves 8.

Vegetable Secrets

Stir-fry Oriental

STEAMED KALE

Eat your greens—at least 1 serving daily! Lance, our chef from the Southern states, taught me how to cook flavorful greens. I had a hard time getting my husband to eat them until he tasted them cooked this way.

- 1 bunch kale—about 12 medium stems (collard greens may be cooked in the same way)
- 1 cup water
- 1 clove garlic (or ¼ teaspoon garlic powder)
- 1 teaspoon onion powder
- 1 tablespoon Bragg Liquid Aminos

1. **Strip kale off the stems.**

    Simply pull leafy part off with your hands and discard the stems.

2. **Place water in a medium-sized saucepan and add the garlic and seasonings; then the kale.**

3. **Bring to a boil and simmer for 30 minutes.**

4. **Serve with Simple Mayonnaise (p. 57) or Tofu Sour Cream (p. 58).**

    ❧*Serves 4-6.*

CHARD OR SPINACH

Chard and spinach require only 5 to 10 minutes' cooking time. For chard, follow same directions as for kale, except after stripping leafy part off the stems of red or white chard, use the stems by cutting in ½-inch slices.

Reduce water to ½ cup and simmer sliced stems for 5 minutes. Meanwhile, slice the leaves in smaller pieces and then add them to the simmering stems and cook for 5 more minutes.

"In order to know what are the best foods, we must study God's original plan for man's diet. He who created man and who understands his needs appointed Adam his food. 'Behold,' He said, 'I have given you every herb yielding seed . . . and every tree, in which is the fruit of a tree yielding seed; to you it shall be for food.' Upon leaving Eden to gain his livelihood by tilling the earth under the curse of sin, man received permission to eat also 'the herb of the field.' "

E. G. White, The Ministry of Healing, *pp. 295, 296*

Curried Rice Pilaf

CURRIED RICE PILAF

This rice dish can be served as a side dish or made into a main dish by adding diced Veggie Cutlets (p. 37) or Soy Curls. Mushrooms make a nice addition.

1 cup diced onion or ¼ dried onion flakes

½ teaspoon salt

4 cups cooked **Fluffy Brown Rice** (p. 49)

1 diced red pepper

1 carrot, shredded

1 cup frozen peas

½ tablespoon curry powder

½ cup diced **Veggie Cutlets** or **Soy Curls** (optional)

1. Place diced onion in a large nonstick skillet over medium-high heat. Add ¼ cup water and salt. Simmer 5 minutes.

2. Add the remaining ingredients. Toss together and heat to serving temperature.

Variation: *Mexican Rice
Replace peas with black beans and corn, and curry powder with* **Homemade Taco Seasoning** *(p. 46).*

VEGETABLE TOFU KEBABS

A fun way to serve your vegetables—adults and children love this colorful combination!

1 cup firm tofu

½ green pepper, cut into 1-inch squares

8 button mushrooms

8 cherry tomatoes

1 small zucchini

Sweet and Sour Marinade: Combine 1 tablespoon **Bragg Liquid Aminos** with 1 tablespoon honey, 1 teaspoon lemon juice, and ½ teaspoon salt.

garlic salt

4 bamboo or metal skewers

1. Place pieces of tofu and vegetables on skewer, then repeat. Brush lightly with Sweet and Sour Marinade. Sprinkle with garlic salt.

2. Cook on a preheated char-grill or barbecue until vegetables are tender. Or place on a nonstick or lightly oiled cookie sheet and bake in the oven at 450°F for about 10 minutes, then on top rack under broiler for 5 minutes.

❧*Serves 4.*

STUFFED BAKED POTATOES WITH CHIPOTLE

2 large hot baked potatoes

4 tablespoons **Simple Butter** (p. 56) (if you don't have Simple Butter on hand, just use 2 tablespoons soy or coconut milk and salt to taste)

1 recipe **Creamy Chipotle Pepper Dressing** (p. 58) or **Tofu Sour Cream** (p. 58)

1 firm-ripe avocado, diced

1 tomato, diced

1. Cut potatoes in half and scoop out the potato. Top with 1 tablespoon Simple Butter and mash lightly with a fork. Add salt if desired.

2. Return potato mixture to potato skin halves. Place in a shallow baking dish and bake at 400°F for 10 minutes.

3. To serve, spoon Creamy Chipotle Pepper Dressing or Tofu Sour Cream over potato and top with diced avocado and tomatoes.

❧*Serves 8.*

"Every 12 minutes someone dies from breast cancer. Yet women who eat as few as two servings of vegetables per day reduce their breast cancer risk by 30 percent."

Annals of the New York Academy of Sciences *768 (1995): 1-11*

"The Lord intends to bring His people back to live upon simple fruits, vegetables, and grains."

E. G. White, Counsels on Diet and Foods, *p. 81*

"Vegetarian diets offer disease protection benefits because of their lower saturated fat, cholesterol, and animal protein content and often higher concentration of folate (which reduces serum homocysteine levels), antioxidants such as vitamins C and E, carotenoids, and phytochemicals."

Journal of the American Dietetic Association *95 (1995): 180-189*

Zucchini Creole

ZUCCHINI CREOLE

8 cups sliced green and yellow zucchini

1 cup diced onion

1 green pepper, diced

1 clove garlic

¾ cup water

1 teaspoon salt

¾ teaspoon Italian seasoning

½ teaspoon dill weed

1 tablespoon Chicken-Like Seasoning

3 cups diced fresh tomatoes

1-2 tablespoons cornstarch dissolved in ¼ cup water

1. Place all ingredients except tomatoes and cornstarch in a saucepan and cook about 8 minutes, until zucchini is tender.

2. Add tomatoes and stir in dissolved cornstarch. Stir as the sauce comes to a boil and thickens. Serve as side dish or over pasta topped with Tofu Sour Cream (p. 58).

☙*Serves 8-10.*

HOLIDAY BAKED YAMS

2 large yams (about 2 pounds)

1 cup raisins

¼ cup pure maple syrup or honey

1 cup soy or coconut milk

1 teaspoon coriander

½ teaspoon each salt and ginger

½ cup pecan halves or pieces

1. Steam yams until thoroughly cooked. Mash peeled yams and all ingredients except pecans, stirring in the amount of milk needed to make a moist texture (or mix milk and syrup with seasonings and raisins, fold into diced yams).

2. Place in a casserole dish and top with pecans. Bake uncovered at 350°F for 20-30 minutes.

☙*Serves 6-8.*

otatoes are the ultimate comfort food, with a long history of keeping famine at bay and families together. There are many varieties of potatoes and an unlimited number of ways to cook them. In recent times, however, the potato has gotten a reputation for being fattening and a food to be avoided by weight watchers. The good news is that potatoes can still be enjoyed in dozens of ways when simply but tastefully prepared.

MASHED POTATOES

See picture, page 41, of a Christmas meal.

8 cups peeled and diced russet or red potatoes

Red potatoes may be cooked and mashed with the skins on. Russet potatoes are best peeled because of the coarse skins.

1 teaspoon salt, or to taste

1 cup cashew or soy or coconut milk

1. Cover potatoes with water and cook for about ½ hour or until very soft.

2. Remove from heat and drain off water.

3. Mash with a potato masher or use an electric mixer. Add milk and salt to taste, adding as much milk as needed for the consistency you like.

Hint: It is important to mash the potatoes immediately after removing from the heat, or they will become starchy and gummy when mashed.

☙*Serves 6-8.*

CREAMED POTATOES AND PEAS

4 cups diced potatoes

½ teaspoon salt

½ recipe **Basic Cream Sauce** (p. 26)

2 cups frozen peas

1. Cook potatoes in 1 cup water with ½ teaspoon salt for 10-15 minutes.

2. Add blended cream sauce and gently stir until thick. Add peas. Serve hot.

Variation: *Make with 2 cups carrots instead of peas. Dice the carrots about half the size of the potatoes and cook with the potatoes with 1 cup diced onion if desired.*

☙*Makes 6 cups.*

Efficiency Tip: Cook a kettleful of potatoes and use in various ways throughout the week—Potato Salad (p. 62), Oven Roasted Potatoes (p. 55), Creamed Potatoes and Peas (p. 55), Hardy Hash (p. 111), Lite Fried Potatoes (p. 55), or French Fries (p. 55).

In a hurry? Slice potatoes or sweet potatoes thin and boil 10 minutes in salted water; drain. Coat with 1 to 2 tablespoons Simple Butter (p. 56), and serve.

FRENCH FRIES

Baked, not fried! See picture on pag 34.

1 large russet baking potato

salt and paprika

1. **Wash potato and slice lengthwise into ½-inch slices. Cut the slices into french fry strips (skin may be left on).**

2. **Place in a Pyrex baking dish or bowl and sprinkle with salt and paprika to taste. Toss until evenly coated.**

3. **Place in microwave and cook for approximately 5 minutes, or until tender but not shriveled or dry.**

Nonmicrowave Option: Steam 10 minutes on the stove.

4. **Place precooked potatoes on a lightly oiled or** Bake Magic-**lined cookie sheet and bake at 450°F for approximately 15 minutes, or until crispy brown and puffy— watch carefully so they don't burn.**

5. **Serve immediately with ketchup or Tofu Sour Cream (p. 58).**

Tip: Potatoes may be baked without precooking in the microwave, eliminating step 3. But precooking speeds the baking and results in a nicer texture and appearance.

OVEN-ROASTED POTATOES

1 pound cooked potatoes

paprika

salt to taste

Other optional seasonings:
   California Chili or seasoned salt
   garlic powder
   fresh rosemary sprigs, chopped

1. **Dice the potatoes in ½-inch cubes, and place in a mixing bowl. Toss with paprika, salt, and other seasonings.**

2. **Place on a nonstick cookie sheet, or on a cookie sheet that is lined with a** Bake Magic **or similar baking sheet.**

3. **Bake at 425°F until golden brown and puffy. Serve hot with ketchup or salsa.**

SCALLOPED POTATOES

Another recipe from Kimberley's kitchen: When she served this to her family, they all agreed that they liked it better than the milk, butter, and cheese recipes they used to eat!

6 cups thinly sliced potatoes

1 onion, sliced in rings

1 can coconut milk (lower fat version: 1 cup each coconut milk and water blended with 2 tablespoons flour)

½ tablespoon onion powder

½ teaspoon garlic powder

1 teaspoon salt

1. **Boil potatoes and onions in 6 cups water with 2 teaspoons salt for 5 minutes. Drain and place in an 8-inch oiled casserole dish.**

2. **Combine milk with seasonings and pour over potatoes, pressing them firmly into the milk. Sprinkle with paprika if desired.**

3. **Bake uncovered at 400°F for 45 minutes.**

☙*Serves 4.*

LITE FRIED POTATOES

This recipe uses the caramelizing technique to flavor both the onions and the potatoes, giving them a delicious fried flavor without the grease.

1 cup diced onion

1 clove garlic or ½ teaspoon garlic powder

½ to 1 teaspoon salt

2 cups diced cooked potatoes

½ teaspoon paprika

1 teaspoon onion powder

1. **Place diced onions in a nonstick skillet with ¼ cup water. Add garlic and salt. Cover, simmer until water is gone and let the onions begin to brown. Add 1-2 tablespoons water and stir, mixing the browned area that has begun to stick to the pan into the water until it dissolves and coats the onions.**

2. **Add the potatoes, paprika, and onion powder. Stir to mix flavorings into the potatoes. Heat until liquid is mostly evaporated. Serve.**

☙*Serves 2-4.*

I consider this section to be a pivotal SECRET to success. Here's why—there are three things we all use on our food that get us into trouble:

butter or margarine

mayonnaise

salad dressing

Butter is trouble because it is an animal fat and high in cholesterol. Margarine, mayonnaise, and salad dressings, with few exceptions, are high in hydrogenated fats or refined oils. But people load up their grocery carts with them and use them on just about everything.

So what's the solution? Find replacements that taste really good. Remember the 'something better' principle: " 'Something better' is the watchword of education, the law of all true living. Whatever Christ asks us to renounce, He offers in its stead something better" (E. G. White, *Education*, p. 296).

If your replacement for butter isn't very buttery, no one will eat it, and you will soon find yourself buying something they *will* eat. It also needs to be simple enough to keep you from feeling overwhelmed and reverting to old habits.

I consider these recipes to be the true "grail" of healthful eating. They are a little richer, but note that the ingredients are largely unrefined, reducing disease-causing risks to a minimum. The calories in spreads that are rich in natural fat are still only a fraction of those contained in their grocery-store counterparts. Family and friends enjoy the food without realizing how healthful it is, because taste and eye appeal have not been sacrificed.

SIMPLE BUTTER

I have tried many variations for a butter replacement, but needed something with ingredients available in Monument Valley and the Caribbean, two places where we've held nutrition seminars, I prayed, and God guided me to this combination. Now it's my favorite—for flavor, texture, and simplicity. (My grandchildren love it too!)

    ¾ cup coconut milk*

    ½ cup water

    2 tablespoons yellow cornmeal

    ½ teaspoon salt, or McCormick's Butter Flavored Salt, or Flavacol Popcorn Salt

*May use ¼ cup unsweetened finely shredded coconut or raw cashew nuts instead of coconut milk, and increase water to 1¼ cups. If you have only sweetened coconut, the sugar can be rinsed out with hot water, using a sieve.

1. Place all ingredients in a saucepan and bring to a boil. Simmer 5 minutes.

It should begin to thicken, about the consistency of thin porridge. I've learned that this can vary with the cornmeal used, so if it isn't getting thick, add another teaspoon of cornmeal and cook a few more minutes until it is like thin pancake batter or porridge.

2. Place in blender, cover, and turn on low, then increase to high. Blend for about 1 minute until as smooth as possible. (If using shredded coconut or cashew nuts, blend for 2 minutes.)

3. Pour into a container; cover and chill. It will be runny, but sets up when cold.

This will keep for about 10 days in the refrigerator, but after a few days it gets stiffer. If this happens, just add a bit of water and stir briskly until soft. I like to make a new batch every week. If there is any of the old still remaining, I stir it into a frozen vegetable dish, such as frozen corn.

Makes 1 cup.

Secrets for Spreads and Salads

Simple Mayonnaise (p. 57) is easy to make but very important—used every day in salads, sandwiches, and spreads. I can't find a good-tasting mayonnaise in the store that doesn't include refined oil or vinegar (also used in the Ranch-style Dressing [p. 57] and in Vegetable Wraps [p. 75]).

SIMPLE MAYONNAISE

12-ounce box MoriNu Silken Soft Tofu, or ½ brick regular tofu plus ¾ cup water

1 cup raw cashew nuts

¼ cup lemon juice

1½ tablespoons honey (or 2 of sugar)

2 teaspoons salt

1 teaspoon onion powder (be sure it is the fine powder, not granulated onion)

Place all ingredients in blender, and blend for at least 1 minute until silky smooth. Chill to thicken.

Tip: Don't underestimate the importance of the right balance of lemon, sweetening, and salt. This is what helps your spread taste like mayonnaise. For low salt, cut salt, sweetener, and lemon juice in half.

✍*Makes 3 cups.*

CREAMY MAYONNAISE

This is a very creamy and simple recipe if you are able to find Soy Supreme easily—see Shopping Secrets (p. 104).

Follow Simple Mayonnaise (above), but replace tofu with ⅔ cup Soy Supreme and 2 cups water. Bring to a boil and chill.

WEIGHT WATCHER'S MAYONNAISE

Follow Simple Mayonnaise (above), but use ⅓ cup raw cashews instead of 1 cup. Add 1-2 tablespoons potato flour and blend together at least 1 minute.

Because this recipe uses fewer cashew nuts, you will need to use potato flour (not potato starch) to make it thick enough (see Glossary [p. 104]).

RICE MAYONNAISE

If tofu or cashews can't be used, try this:

Follow Simple Mayonnaise (above), but instead of tofu and cashews, use 1 can coconut milk and 1¼ cups hot, well-cooked rice or millet. Blend for about 2 minutes until silky smooth. Chill to thicken.

RANCH-STYLE DRESSING

1 cup mayonnaise of choice

1 tablespoon lemon juice (optional)

¼ cup water

1 rounded tablespoon **Ranch-style Dressing Mix** (see tip below or recipe following)

Mix all ingredients together in a small bowl and serve with tossed salad.

Tip: You can buy regular packaged dressing mix to use here. But when you have the time, the homemade mix below is simple to make and much less expensive.

RANCH-STYLE DRESSING MIX

¼ cup onion powder

1 tablespoon celery salt or Vege-Sal

2 tablespoons dried parsley flakes

1 tablespoon poppy seeds

1 tablespoon dill weed

2 teaspoons garlic powder

2 teaspoons sweet basil

1½ teaspoons salt

1 tablespoon sugar

Mix together and store in an airtight container.

✍*Makes 1 cup.*

Crispy Baked Tortilla Chips

Tofu Sour Cream

CREAMY CHIPOTLE PEPPER DRESSING

Kimberley developed this recipe to use on Fiesta Salad (p. 44) and Stuffed Baked Potatoes With Chipoltle (p. 52). Good on burgers, sandwiches, as a dip for French Fries (p. 55), carrot sticks, and just about anything!

- 1 red, yellow, or orange pepper, cut in half (may use green pepper)
- 2-3 tablespoons sweet or green onion, chopped very fine
- 1-2 tablespoons fresh cilantro, chopped very fine
- ½ teaspoon cumin
- ¼ teaspoon garlic powder
- ½ teaspoon **Wright's Hickory Seasoning**
- 1 tablespoon tomato paste (you can use 2 tablespoons barbecue sauce instead of the Wright's seasoning and tomato paste)
- 1 recipe Tofu Sour Cream (p. 58)

1. Arrange pepper halves on a cookie sheet, skin side up, and place under broiler. Broil until skin is black. Peel skin off and dice peppers into small pieces (or save time and chop raw).

2. Mix peppers and all other ingredients together with Tofu Sour Cream. Chill and use when needed.

❧Makes 2 cups.

TOFU SOUR CREAM

This recipe is almost the same as Simple Mayonnaise (p. 57), but uses no sweetener and less lemon juice and salt. Use on baked potatoes, Cuban Black Beans (p. 49), Stacked Enchilada Bake (p. 47), or any place you would use sour cream.

- 1 12-ounce box **MoriNu Silken Soft Tofu**, or 9 ounces regular tofu and ½ cup water
- ½ cup raw cashew nuts
- 1 tablespoon lemon juice
- 1 teaspoon salt
- 1 teaspoon onion powder
- 2 tablespoons snipped fresh chives (may use dried chives)

1. Place all ingredients in blender, except the chives. Blend for at least 1 minute until silky smooth.

2. Add the chives. (Blend briefly or green sour cream will result.) Serve (thickens more if chilled).

Variation: *Dill Dressing*
Blend in ½ teaspoon each dill weed, Italian seasoning and garlic powder, 1 tablespoon sugar, and more salt to taste (about 1 teaspoon). Add a little water to achieve desired consistency.

❧Makes 2 cups.

HUMUS TAHINI

Our friends from the Middle East use this simple topping with their pita and so do we. But a good slice of whole wheat bread is a perfect companion for this wonderful spread. If you don't have sesame tahini, you can use toasted sesame seeds. We have made this in countries where the best nut available was peanuts, and we all loved it. Try it sometime— just replace the sesame tahini with ½ cup dry-roasted peanuts or raw cashews. A different flavor that many have told us they like better than tahini!

- 2 cups cooked garbanzos (15-ounce can)
- 2 tablespoons sesame tahini
- 2 tablespoons lemon juice
- 1 clove garlic or ½ teaspoon garlic powder
- salt to taste (½ to 1 teaspoon)
- ½ teaspoon cumin
- ½ to 1 cup water (or juice from canned garbanzos)
- 6-8 sprigs fresh cilantro leaves (optional)

Blend all together, except cilantro, adding water in the amount needed to the thickness desired. Blend until smooth, about 1 minute. Add cilantro leaves and blend briefly—just enough to chop.

❧Makes 3 cups.

APRICOT-PINEAPPLE SPREAD

This spread never lasts long at our table because it's such a favorite!

- 1 cup dried apricots
- 1 cup pineapple juice
- 2 cups crushed pineapple canned in juice
- ¼ cup honey (optional)

1. Place apricots and pineapple juice in blender and blend briefly to chop fine.

2. Place in a saucepan with the crushed pineapple and bring to a boil. Simmer 5 minutes. Add honey, if needed, to taste. Chill to serve.

Variation: *Blend all ingredients until smooth, adding more apricots as needed until you achieve a spreadable consistency. Serve uncooked.*

Tip: This same idea can be used with any dried fruit and juice to make a nice fruit spread for muffins, rolls, or toast.

Makes 4 cups.

PRUNE-APPLE BUTTER

A recipe with simple ingredients, easily available.

- 2 cups diced, unskinned raw apples*
- ¾ cup water
- ½ teaspoon coriander
- 1 teaspoon maple flavoring
- 1 cup or more dried pitted prunes

*Instead of apples and water, you can use 1 cup applesauce. A little pure maple syrup is a nice addition if it needs sweetening.

1. Cut and core apples and place in blender along with the water. Blend together until smooth.

2. Add the flavorings and the prunes, adding more or less prunes to make the consistency of a spreadable butter.

3. Serve right away or cook by placing in a nonstick kettle and bringing to a boil—then reduce heat and simmer for about 10 minutes. If you don't cook the butter, eat it within a few days (otherwise freeze it, lest it ferment).

Cooked prune butter will keep several weeks. It can also be poured into hot sterilized jars and sealed.

Makes 2½ cups.

FRESH RASPBERRY JAM

The secret to this delicious jam is the uncooked fresh berry taste. The secret ingredient is Instant Clear Jel. Other berries or fruits may be used.

- 2 cups frozen raspberries (1 cup thawed)
- 1 cup frozen apple juice concentrate, thawed
- 2 tablespoons honey (optional)
- 2 tablespoons Instant Clear Jel

1. Place all ingredients in blender in order given. Add Clear Jel carefully so it doesn't stick to the sides of the blender.

2. Cover blender and turn on low for about 3 seconds—just enough for everything to go through the blades and mix in the jel. Too much blending makes the berry seeds separate and doesn't look as nice.

3. Remove to a container and chill. It will get thicker as it sits.

Tip: Don't have Clear Jel? Use 2½ tablespoons cornstarch dissolved in a small amount of the apple juice. Add the rest of the apple juice and juice drained from the thawed berries. (Don't add the berries yet.) Bring the juice to a boil while stirring. Cool in the refrigerator for about an hour and then stir in the berries.

Makes 3 cups.

Citrus Walnut Tossed Salad

CITRUS WALNUT TOSSED SALAD

Sweet, tart, and crunchy gourmet salad.

2 oranges (1 small can whole mandarin orange segments may be used instead)

1 cup sugar snap peas, ends and strings removed

6-8 cups romaine lettuce, bite-sized pieces (or use part green leaf lettuce or mixed salad greens)

1 cup sliced cucumber

½ cup walnuts or Honey-roasted Walnuts (p. 60)

1. Peel the oranges, removing all the white pith. Cut the fruit into segments between the membrane, removing any seeds.

2. Cover the sugar snap peas with boiling water and let stand for 2 minutes. Plunge the peas into iced water. Drain and pat dry.

3. Combine lettuce, peas, oranges, cucumber, and walnuts in a bowl. Toss with Raspberry Dressing (p. 60) and serve.

꙳*Serves 6-8.*

HONEY-ROASTED WALNUTS

½ tablespoon water

1 tablespoon honey

¼ teaspoon salt or butter-flavored salt

2 cups walnut halves (or almonds or pecans)

Combine water, honey, and salt in a bowl. Add the walnuts and stir together. Spread walnuts onto a cookie sheet. Place in oven at 350°F for 10 minutes.

RASPBERRY DRESSING

1 cup frozen or fresh raspberries*

½ cup apple juice concentrate*

2 teaspoons cornstarch dissolved in ½ cup water

1 tablespoon lemon juice

2 tablespoons honey

1 teaspoon salt

1½ teaspoons basil

1. Heat berries and strain through a sieve to remove seeds.

2. Pour juice into a saucepan with remaining ingredients and stir while bringing to a boil. Chill.

May use ¾ cup raspberry-apple or cranberry-apple juice concentrate in place of the berries and apple juice, but it's better made with fresh or frozen berries.

꙳*Makes 1½ cups.*

MARINATED CUCUMBER SALAD

My husband is always pleased when I serve him this salad. It's his mother's recipe!

6 cups cucumber slices

½ cup orange juice concentrate

¾ teaspoon dill weed

1 teaspoon salt

1 teaspoon onion powder

¼ teaspoon garlic powder

1. Peel cucumbers and, if desired, score with the tines of a fork; slice thinly. Combine with all other ingredients.

3. Place in a covered container and leave overnight in the refrigerator to marinate. Keeps for at least a week.

꙳*Serves 6-8.*

Basic Tossed Green Salad

I like to buy a small head of purple cabbage and keep it on hand to mix into a tossed salad. It keeps for weeks, and a little shredded purple cabbage with the dark romaine is full of eye appeal. Add to that some red tomato wedges, and you have a beautiful gourmet salad. Other vegetables such as cucumbers may be added if you have them.

6-8 cups romaine lettuce, cut or torn into bite-sized pieces (*or use part iceberg or green leaf lettuce*)

¼ cup finely shredded purple cabbage

2 small tomatoes, diced or cut in wedges

Ways to dress or serve the salad:

1. Serve with Ranch-style Dressing (p. 57) on the side.

2. Serve with dressing already mixed in. Fold into your salad about ¼ cup Simple Mayonnaise (p. 57) and 1 tablespoon Ranch-style Dressing Mix (p. 57). Serve in a clean bowl.

3. Stir in about ¼ cup pineapple-orange juice concentrate, and a few shakes each of dill weed, basil, garlic, and onion powder, and salt or seasoned salt. Good with diced avocado.

 Serves 6-8.

Asian Cucumber Salad

Here's another way to flavor cucumbers—Kimberley introduced us to this one. We have served it to crowds of people with great success.

4 cups sliced cucumbers

1 tablespoon lemon juice

4-5 drops sesame oil (optional)

2 tablespoons Bragg Liquid Aminos

2 tablespoons chopped fresh cilantro leaves

1 clove garlic, crushed

½ tablespoon finely chopped peanuts or peanut butter

1 tablespoon roasted sesame seeds

¼ cup finely sliced red onion

Mix all together and serve.

 Serves 4-6.

Cucumber Chips
(Fresh Sweet Pickles)

If you are looking for a good-tasting pickle without vinegar, here's your answer. It's simple to make, crunchy, and delicious in sandwiches!

½ cup apple juice concentrate

2 tablespoons lemon juice

2 cloves garlic, crushed

1 tablespoon honey

1½ teaspoons salt

½ teaspoon dill weed

½ teaspoon onion powder

1 medium cucumber

1. Place all ingredients except cucumbers in a large skillet and bring to a boil. Meanwhile, slice the cucumber in whole, round slices, skin included. Add to the boiling juice, cover, and bring to a boil. Remove cover and stir, then cover again and leave on heat for about 30 seconds more. Don't overcook.

2. Remove from heat and let sit uncovered for 5 minutes. Place in a covered storage container and chill for several hours or overnight.

3. Drain off the liquid and use chilled Cucumber Chips in burgers and sandwiches.

 Makes 1 quart.

Tip: Liquid can be made into a delicious salad dressing. Just place in blender with ½ cup raw cashew nuts or 2 tablespoons sesame tahini. Blend smooth. Good on tossed salad or as a dressing for coleslaw.

Asian Cucumber

Creamy Waldorf

CREAMY WALDORF SALAD

6 Fuji apples (Red or Golden Delicious are next-best)

1 cup diced celery

1 cup raisins or sliced, pitted dates

¾ cup coarsely chopped roasted almonds, cashew nuts, or walnuts

1½ cups **Whipped Topping** (p. 99)

1 tablespoon fresh lemon juice

1. **Quarter and core apples. Slice each quarter into five or six thin slices and cut slices in half. Place apples in a mixing bowl and toss with fresh lemon juice to keep from browning.**

2. **Slice celery in thin diagonal slices and add to apples.**

3. **Add remaining ingredients. Serve as is or chill.**

Serves 8-10.

POTATO SALAD

10 cups diced potatoes cooked in 6 cups water with 1 tablespoon salt; drain

Blend together and bring to boil:

1 cup coconut milk

¾ cup water

½ cup cashew nuts

1 tablespoon lemon juice

1 tablespoon sugar

1½ teaspoons salt

1 teaspoon each onion powder and **Chicken-Like Seasoning**

2 tablespoons Soy Supreme or soy milk powder (or omit and increase cashews to ¾ cup)

Combine potatoes with blended mix and chill. Then add:

½ teaspoon dill weed

1 small grated carrot or diced red pepper

1 cup diced celery

1 or 2 diced dill pickles

Makes 10 cups.

COLESLAW

½ head cabbage, shredded

1 carrot, shredded

1 small can crushed pineapple

½ teaspoon salt

½ cup **Simple or Creamy Mayonnaise** (p. 57)

1 tablespoon honey (optional)

Mix all together and serve. Marinating for a day in the refrigerator will enhance the flavor.

Makes 4 cups.

CARROT AND RAISIN SALAD

Same as Coleslaw—except use 2 cups shredded carrots instead of cabbage, and ½ cup raisins.

Variation: *Broccoli*
Replace carrots with 4 cups finely chopped broccoli and add: ¼ cup toasted pine nuts or sunflower seeds and 1 tablespoon chopped cilantro.

BERRY-CRANBERRY LAYERED FRUIT SALAD

1½ cups water

2 teaspoons agar powder

12-ounce can frozen white grape juice concentrate

1½ cups frozen mixed berries such as raspberries, blackberries, strawberries, etc., crushed (measure berries when frozen)

½ cup fresh or frozen cranberries (or increase mixed berries to 2 cups)

½ cup crushed pineapple with juice

1 small apple, finely chopped

2 tablespoons honey or sugar if needed, depending on tartness of berries

2 cups Whipped Topping (p. 99)

1. **Place water in a small saucepan and stir in agar powder. Bring to a boil, reduce heat and simmer for 1-2 minutes.**

2. **Combine remaining ingredients (except Whipped Topping), including boiled agar mixture. Chill 2-4 hours.**

3. **In six dessert goblets, alternate layers of fruit mixture with Whipped Topping. For large trifle bowl, double recipe. Chill and serve.**

Tips: Instead of layering in a trifle bowl or goblets, use a flat glass casserole dish and top with a layer of Whipped Topping.

Variation: *Other juice may be used, such as apple, or white grape raspberry.*

Some prefer agar because it is not an animal product but if you don't have agar, use regular gelatin or 1½ tablespoons of Knox Unflavored Gelatin and simply bring to a boil in step 1.

"To cook well, to present healthful food upon the table in an inviting manner, requires intelligence and experience. The one who prepares the food that is to be placed in our stomachs, to be converted into blood to nourish the system, occupies a most important and elevated position."

E. G. White, Counsels on Diet and Foods, p. 252

Bread,
Soup,
and
Sandwiches

YEAST BREAD

We are blessed in most parts of this country with good whole grain bread. So why add to our busy lives the extra burden of baking bread? Maybe this section is for those who find pleasure and satisfaction in mixing the dough, watching it rise, placing it in the oven, and filling the house with the wonderful aroma of fresh-baked bread. It's extra easy if you have a bread machine—the kind that makes and bakes one loaf. Here is our "secret" recipe for moist and light whole wheat bread, and lots of ways to use that exciting little ball of dough!

ONE LOAF BREAD

This bread recipe is the right amount for one loaf, and works in most bread machines. The following pages feature lots of delicious breads based on this little ball of dough.

> 1½ cups warm water
>
> 2 tablespoons applesauce
>
> 2 tablespoons honey
>
> 1 teaspoon salt
>
> 2 teaspoons active dry yeast
>
> 3 cups whole wheat bread flour
>
> 1 tablespoon gluten flour
>
> 1 tablespoon dough conditioner
> (optional)

Place ingredients in container according to manufacturer's instructions.

PITA (POCKET) BREAD

Why do we include a recipe for pita bread when you can buy it—whole wheat, too? Because the pocket bread you make is so much better! And it's really fun and easy to make—especially if you have a bread machine. Once you start making your own, you and your family will be spoiled. Fresh homemade pocket bread is softer and more pliable, and, unlike the ones you buy, doesn't tear when you fill it.

1. **Place a layer of quarry tiles on the bottom rack of your oven and preheat to 450°F. (Tiles can be purchased at flooring stores or large home improvement stores. They usually come in 12-inch or 6-inch squares, and are reddish-brick color and about ½ inch thick. Don't get glazed tiles—just the natural surface.)**

Don't try to skip this important secret to making pita that forms a pocket every time!

2. **Follow directions for One Loaf Bread (p. 64), removing dough when it has been kneaded. Go to step 4 to make the dough into pita bread. If kneading by hand, place water, applesauce, and honey in a mixing bowl and sprinkle the yeast on top. Let sit 5 minutes. The mixture should be warm, about 100°F.**

3. **Stir, then knead in the flour and salt, adding more or less flour as needed to make a ball of dough that can be kneaded for about 10 minutes.**

4. **Divide dough into eight pieces, kneading each into a smooth ball.**

5. **Roll each ball into a circle about ¼ inch thick. It helps to flatten the ball first with your hands, and then coat the top with flour so that it doesn't stick to your rolling pin as you roll it out.**

6. **You will need three or four cookie sheets, turned upside down. Dust the bottom of each finished circle with plenty of flour, and place on the upside-down cookie sheet to rise until almost double (about 30-45 minutes—depending on how warm the room is).**

7. **Place two or three at a time on hot tiles, transferring them carefully with a metal spatula and slipping them quickly onto the tile.**

Close oven door and time for 4 minutes. They should puff up like a balloon. At

this high temperature, they bake very quickly. Remove and bake the next ones, repeating until all are finished.

8. Cool on a rack for about 10 minutes, then cut in half with a sharp knife and place in plastic bags immediately to prevent them from drying out. Freeze any that are not used within a day or two.

PUMPKIN-ORANGE-RAISIN BREAD

My husband is a raisin lover, and when it comes to bread—well, it just isn't bread if it doesn't have raisins in it. The orange not only gives a wonderful flavor, but the ascorbic acid in the orange makes lighter bread. I make it in a Bosch bread machine, but it can be made by hand. This recipe makes six or seven loaves: some to eat, some to freeze, and some to give away!

> 4 cups warm water
>
> 1 cup canned pumpkin (may use 1½ cups cooked squash)
>
> ¼ cup honey or scant ½ cup sugar
>
> 1 whole orange, including half the peel
>
> 3 tablespoons instant dry yeast
>
> ½ cup gluten flour
>
> ½ cup dough conditioner (optional)
>
> 10-12 cups whole wheat bread flour
>
> 1½ tablespoons salt
>
> 5 cups raisins

1. Place 2 cups water in a blender along with the pumpkin, honey, whole orange cut in several pieces, and with half of the orange peel. Blend for 1 minute. Add remaining water, as needed, to blend freely. Measure total amount of liquid, adding more water until there is 7 cups total mixture.

2. Place blended liquid in a mixing bowl and add yeast, gluten flour, dough conditioner (if you use it), and 6 cups of the flour. Beat with a wooden spoon for about 3 minutes or in a bread machine with a dough hook. Cover and let rise as a soft sponge until double.

3. Beat down and add the salt, raisins, and remaining flour in the amount needed to make a dough that can be kneaded by hand for about 15 minutes, or in your mixer for 10 minutes.

4. Shape into six or seven loaves and let rise until double. Place in 400°F, preheated oven. Turn down to 350°F and bake for 40 minutes or until golden brown.

Variation: *Orange Bread*
Leave out the raisins and replace pumpkin with applesauce. Makes a delicious, moist, fragrant orange bread.

PIZZA CRUST

Divide One Loaf Bread (p. 64) dough into two balls, and roll each into a 12-inch circle. Stretch onto an oiled pizza pan. Spread with warm Simple Cheese Sauce (p. 26) and tomato sauce (see p. 30) and let rise in a warm place for about 40 minutes. Bake at 350°F for 30 minutes or until crust is golden brown.

Freeze crusts for future use. After rolling out the crusts, stretch onto oiled pizza pan, pierce with a fork in several places, and let rise in a warm place until double —about 45 minutes. Bake at 350°F for about 10 minutes. Cool on a rack, then wrap in plastic and freeze for future use.

SWEET ROLLS

1. **Make** One Loaf Bread (p. 64) dough and roll out into a long rectangle. Apply a thin layer of Date Spread (below) over the surface, leaving ¼ inch along one long edge free of spread.

2. Sprinkle entire surface liberally with raisins. (Dried cranberries and other diced dried fruits make it extra-special!) Roll up the long way like a jelly roll, and pinch the seam closed.

3. Cut 1-inch rolls by cutting all the way through with a sharp knife or scissors. Place rolls with cut side up on a lightly oiled cookie sheet, shaping into a circle and flattening slightly with hands. Let rise in a warm place for about an hour or until doubled.

4. Bake at 350°F for about 20 minutes or until lightly browned. Lightly brush tops with pure maple syrup while hot (optional). Cool on a wire rack, then place in an airtight container until ready to eat.

☙*Makes 20 rolls.*

DATE SPREAD

> 2½ cups date pieces
>
> 1 cup water
>
> 1 teaspoon vanilla
>
> ¼ teaspoon lemon extract, optional
>
> ¼ teaspoon salt

Bring all ingredients to a boil and mash to make a thick paste. Or blend in blender or food processor, adding a little extra water if needed to blend thick and smooth.

Stuffed Italian Bread

STUFFED ITALIAN BREAD

This recipe has been so well received that I have used it again and again. It's great with soup or pasta.

One Loaf Bread (p. 64)

Spinach Filling (p. 67)

1. Make One Loaf Bread recipe and remove from machine after it kneeds, or mix and knead by hand.

2. After dough has been kneaded, divide into two pieces. Roll out first piece on a floured surface into a large rectangle and place on an oiled 12" x 17" cookie sheet (half sheet pan) that has sides. Stretch dough to the sides of the pan and press against the sides to secure into place, as you would a pizza crust.

3. Spread Spinach Filling over the surface of the dough, about ¼ inch thick, but leaving a small ¼-inch border of the dough free from filling.

4. Roll out remaining piece of dough and place over the top of the filling,

pressing the edges together to form a large stuffed pizza. Prick with a fork over the entire surface.

5. Put in a warm place and let rise for about 1 hour.

Tip: Press dough lightly. Indentation remains when ready to bake.

6. Bake at 350°F for about 30 minutes (lightly browned). Remove and brush lightly with olive oil and sprinkle with garlic salt if desired. Or to season the top without oil: sprinkle with garlic salt and then mist lightly with water from a spray bottle. Cut into squares when cool.

BREADSTICKS

Make One Loaf Bread dough (p. 64) and divide into 16 pieces. Roll each piece into a rope about ½ inch in diameter. Place on a cookie sheet and let rise until double. Bake at 350°F for about 15 minutes or until golden brown. Mist lightly and sprinkle with garlic salt. Serve with soup or with a dip such as guacamole or pasta sauce.

CHEDDA POLENTA

Here's a delicious cheese recipe with simple ingredients using peanuts (cheaper and easier to find than cashews). The ingredients are blended and then baked. When chilled, it becomes firm enough to slice or shred.

1 cup water

½ cup cornmeal

½ cup raw cashew nuts or dry roasted peanuts

3 tablespoons pimentos or 1 teaspoon paprika

1 teaspoon salt

1 teaspoon onion powder

¼ teaspoon garlic powder

1 teaspoon lemon juice

½ tablespoon food yeast flakes (optional)

1. Place all ingredients into a blender and blend for at least 1 minute until completely smooth.

2. Pour into a lightly oiled or nonstick small loaf pan; cover and bake at 350°F for 45 minutes.

3. Cool and slice for sandwiches or crackers. May be shredded and served on top of Fiesta Salad (p. 44).

CALZONES

One Loaf Bread dough (p. 64)*

2 cups warm filling such as Spinach Filling (p. 67), Cutlet Salad Filling (p. 74), or Egglike Salad Sandwich filling (p. 75)

¼ cup Nondairy Parmesan Cheese (p. 67)

1 teaspoon honey dissolved in 2 tablespoons water

1. Roll dough into a 15" x 10" rectangle. Cut rectangle into six 5-inch squares.

Use a ruler to do this. Don't try to guess.

2. Divide filling among squares and brush the edges with water. Lift one corner and stretch dough over to the opposite corner. Press edges of the dough with a fork to seal.

3. Arrange calzones on a greased baking sheet. Prick tops with a fork. Brush tops lightly with the honey-and-water mixture, using a pastry brush. Sprinkle with Nondairy Parmesan Cheese.

4. Bake in a 425°F oven about 10 minutes or till golden brown. Check them after they have baked 8 minutes, and keep checking. They brown quickly.

Good served with spaghetti sauce. If cool or frozen, reheat in oven or toaster.

*Variation: *Instead of bread dough, try a double recipe of* **Cobbler Crust** *(p. 88).*

🍂*Makes 6 calzones.*

SPINACH FILLING

1 cup (8 ounce) firm tofu, crumbled

½ cup Cashew Cream (p. 107) (or Simple Mayonnaise [p. 57]and omit salt)

1 teaspoon salt

½ teaspoon basil

1 tablespoon dried onion flakes

1 teaspoon lemon juice

5 ounces drained, chopped spinach

Combine and mix in small bowl.

Hint: This filling is also good in manicotti or lasagna. See variation on p. 31.

NONDAIRY PARMESAN CHEESE

Do you like to sprinkle Parmesan cheese on pasta dishes? Here's a nondairy version you can make. It keeps for months in the refrigerator, and is a good multipurpose flavoring to spark up many dishes. Good on toast or French bread too!

½ cup yeast flakes

½ cup ground sesame seeds

2 teaspoon garlic powder

1 teaspoon onion powder

1 tablespoon Chicken-Like Seasoning

1 tablespoon lemon juice

Mix together all ingredients and store in an airtight container in the refrigerator.

Hint: the best way to grind sesame seeds is in a small electric seed or coffee mill.

Calzones

Potato Carrot Swirl

Simple. Beautiful. Delicious. Here's a way to make your family or guests feel really special. Serve this gourmet soup with whole wheat french bread and salad or with sandwiches.

> 2 large russet potatoes (4 medium), peeled and cut in large pieces
>
> 1 medium onion, diced
>
> 4 teaspoons Chicken-Like Seasoning
>
> ½ teaspoon salt
>
> 4 medium carrots, peeled and cut in 1-inch pieces
>
> 2 teaspoons curry powder or Homemade Curry Powder (p. 33)
>
> ½ teaspoon salt
>
> 1 can coconut milk (or 2 cups soy or cashew milk)
>
> ½ teaspoon dill weed (or a sprig of fresh dill weed)

1. **Place potatoes, onion, and seasonings in a medium saucepan and add 2 cups water (or enough water to come just below the top of the vegetables).**

2. **In a separate saucepan, place carrots and seasonings, and enough water to reach just below the top of the carrots.**

3. **Bring both to a boil and then simmer for about 20 minutes, or until tender.**

4. **When both are finished cooking, place about one fourth of the potato mixture into the carrot pot, and place remaining potato mixture in blender. Add ½ can coconut milk (or 1 cup soy or cashew milk) and dill weed. Blend on low, adding enough water to bring to desired consistency. The soup will thicken if it sits—simply place on low heat in a covered saucepan.**

5. **Place carrot mixture (with the added potato mixture) into blender. Add the remaining coconut milk and blend on medium until smooth. Add water for desired consistency for the same thickness as the potato soup. Pour back into the other saucepan and place on low heat.**

Tip: Taste both soups, adding more salt if needed.

6. **Using a ladle for each soup, pour both slowly into a wide shallow soup bowl until full. Soup will be half orange and half white. Use a spoon to create a swirl between colors. Garnish with fresh dill (optional) and serve.**

❧Makes 10 cups (5 each), serves 4-6.

PASTA FAGIOLI SOUP

This delicious Italian "bean and pasta" soup makes a nice variation from the more common minestrone soup or chili. Serve with Stuffed Italian Bread (p. 66) and a salad for a complete and hearty meal.

> 1 onion, diced
>
> 4-6 cloves garlic, pressed (1-2 tablespoons)
>
> 3 stalks celery, sliced thin
>
> 2 cups shredded carrots
>
> 4 cups water
>
> 4 teaspoons Italian seasoning
>
> 4-6 sun dried tomatoes, chopped
>
> 1½ teaspoon salt
>
> 1 tablespoon Beef-Like Seasoning
>
> 2 tablespoons onion powder
>
> 1 tablespoon lemon juice

1. **Bring the above ingredients to a boil, reduce heat, and allow the soup to simmer for 15 minutes. Then add:**

> 4 cups water
>
> 2 15-ounce cans crushed tomatoes
>
> 2 15-ounce cans tomato sauce
>
> ¼ cup molasses or 3 tablespoons sugar
>
> 1 can small red beans, rinsed and drained
>
> 1 can navy beans, rinsed and drained
>
> 1 cup veggie burger or other ground beef substitute (see p. 35)

2. **As soon as the soup is boiling again, add:**

> 2 cups small pasta, such as shells or tiny tubes

3. **Simmer for an additional 15 minutes.**

❧Serves 10-12.

Armenian Lentil Soup

Lentils and rice make this soup a satisfying main dish. Spinach and tomatoes are added after the cooking is completed to keep their distinct green and red color, and give the soup eye appeal.

- 1½ cups lentils
- 10 cups water
- ½ cup brown rice
- 1 cup diced onions
- 2 tablespoons lemon juice
- 2 tablespoons Bragg Liquid Aminos
- 1 tablespoon onion powder
- 1 tablespoon salt
- 1 tablespoon Chicken-Like Seasoning
- 1 teaspoon garlic powder
- 1 teaspoon dill weed
- 2 teaspoons cumin
- 1 cup frozen chopped spinach
- 15-ounce can diced tomatoes

1. **Place all ingredients in kettle except spinach and tomatoes. Bring to a boil, reduce heat, and simmer for 1 hour or until lentils are tender.**

2. **Add spinach and simmer 1 minute. Add the tomatoes just before serving. Especially good served with pocket bread and avocados or Humus Tahini (p. 58).**

Makes 12 cups.

Avocado Dip

The surprise ingredient in this recipe is water chestnuts. They give it a fresh crunch that goes well with the sweet onion and tomatoes. Good in pita bread or wraps, or with tortilla chips or crackers.

- 1 large avocado
- 1 teaspoon lime juice
- 2 roma tomatoes (or 1 large tomato, seeded)
- 1 small can water chestnuts
- ½ cup diced, sweet onion
- 12 medium pitted olives, halved
- 3 tablespoons chopped, fresh cilantro
- ½ teaspoon garlic powder
- ¼ cup Simple Mayonnaise (p. 57)
- ½ teaspoon salt, or to taste

"Let us make intelligent advancement in simplifying our diet. In the providence of God, every country produces articles of food containing the nourishment necessary for the upbuilding of the system. These may be made into healthful, appetizing dishes."

E. G. White, Counsels on Diet and Foods, p. 94

1. **Dice avocados and place in a mixing bowl. Add the lime juice, stirring gently to coat the avocados.**

2. **Dice the tomatoes, water chestnuts, and sweet onion, adding them to the avocado mixture along with the olives, chopped cilantro, and garlic powder.**

3. **Gently fold in the Simple Mayonnaise so the avocado retains its shape and is not mashed, adding salt as needed to taste. Refrigerate until needed.**

Makes 4 cups.

Armenian Lentil

Cream of Vegetable with Broccoli

COCONUT CORN CHOWDER

Kimberley likes to make her cream soups by blending a can of coconut milk with 2 cups cooked potatoes. Simmer vegetables with seasonings and add the blended sauce. This corn chowder is an example.

5 cups diced potatoes

1 cup diced onion

1 teaspoon Chicken-Like Seasoning

1 teaspoon onion powder

1 teaspoon butter flavored salt or salt

2 cups water

4 cups frozen corn

½ teaspoon dill weed

1 can coconut milk

1. Place potatoes, onions, and seasonings (except dill weed) in the water and simmer for 15 minutes or until tender.

2. Remove 2 cups of the cooked potatoes with a slotted spoon (you will get some of the onions too, but that's all right), and place in blender. Stir the frozen corn and dill weed into the kettle of soup. Turn off heat while blending the sauce.

2. Add coconut milk to the blender with the cooked potatoes. Blend for about 30 seconds—just until smooth, but not starchy.

3. Add blended mixture to the soup. May add more water or salt as needed to taste. Heat to serving temperature.

Variation: *If you don't want to use coconut milk but like the idea of thickening your soup with blended potato, there are other options. Replace the coconut milk (1 can is a scant 2 cups) with soy milk, or blend ¾ cup cashew nuts with 2 cups water, or use ½ can (1 cup) coconut milk for lower fat soup.*

Makes 8 cups.

CREAM OF VEGETABLE SOUP

Create your own soup with the Basic Cream Sauce!

6 cups diced vegetables*

1 cup water

1 tablespoon Chicken-Like Seasoning

1 teaspoon salt (or more to taste)

½ teaspoon garlic powder

½ teaspoon basil (optional)

1 recipe Basic Cream Sauce (p. 26) or Simple Cheese Sauce (p. 26)

*Good combinations are:

broccoli, onion, and red pepper

corn (4 cups) and diced potatoes (2 cups)—corn chowder!

carrots, cabbage, potatoes, and beets with a little dill weed—borscht!

potatoes and leeks or onions

1. Cook vegetables in 1 cup water with the seasonings, simmering until tender.

2. Meanwhile, blend the Basic Cream Sauce ingredients until very smooth—about 2 minutes.

3. Add Basic Cream Sauce to the cooked vegetables, and stir gently while bringing to a boil to thicken, adding more water or salt as needed.

Makes 8 cups.

BRUSSELS SPROUT SOUP

8-10 Brussels sprouts (or similar amount of cabbage)

½ onion

4-5 fresh mushrooms

1 carrot

4 cups water

2 tablespoons Bragg Liquid Aminos or soy sauce

1 large clove garlic, crushed

1 teaspoon onion powder

1 teaspoon Italian seasoning or dill weed

1 tablespoon Beef-Like Seasoning

½ teaspoon salt

1. Finely slice the Brussels sprouts, onion, and mushrooms. Shred the carrot. (A food processor works good for this!) You should have 4 cups of vegetables when all are sliced and shredded.

2. Place all ingredients in a kettle and bring to a boil. Reduce heat and simmer for 10 minutes.

☙Makes 6 cups.

GOLDEN VEGETABLE SOUP

Here's Kathy's favorite soup. She is a busy mother of three, and this is a recipe she developed over time to delight her children (they like the shells) and herself (easy to make). She took it to a soup potluck recently, and was the only one with an empty soup crock to take home.

1 onion, diced

1 cup shredded carrots (2-3 large)

3 cups diced potatoes

2 teaspoons salt

4 cups water

2 cups pasta shells

1 bunch green onions, diced

1 cup frozen corn

1 can coconut milk (or 1 cup raw cashew nuts and 1½ cups water)

10-ounce can tomato soup (may use 15-ounce can tomatoes in juice)

1 tablespoon Chicken-Like Seasoning

½ teaspoon basil

½ teaspoon dill weed

1 bunch cilantro leaves

1. Place onion, carrots, potatoes, salt, and water in a soup pot and bring to a boil. Reduce heat and simmer 8 minutes.

2. Add pasta shells, diced green onions, and remaining seasonings. Simmer 8 more minutes.

3. Blend coconut milk (or cashew nuts), tomato soup, and corn in blender until smooth. Add to soup along with cilantro leaves and heat to serving temperature.

Hint: It's a tedious job picking all those cilantro leaves off the stems. Kathy says she does that job while talking on the phone to a friend. The bright-green leaves floating in the soup are very pretty, but if you don't have time for that, just cut most of the stems off the bunch of cilantro, and put the tops in the blender after blending the corn mixture. Turn on a few seconds, just enough to chop the cilantro coarsely.

☙*Makes 12 cups.*

Variation: *Also nice with 1 cup frozen peas thawed and added just before serving.*

Open-face Sandwiches

This is the simplest way to enjoy your favorite kind of bread with a good filling or dip. Some of our meals consist of just a hearty bowl of soup, some sliced whole wheat or rye bread, sliced avocado, and a dish of Simple Mayonnaise (p. 57). We usually toast the bread and arrange our fixings on it as we eat.

If we don't have avocado, some of our favorite spreads are Humus Tahini (p. 58) or Spinach Filling (p. 67). Or pictured below, Mock Salmon Spread and Almond-Olive Spread.

Use any of the open-face fillings in pocket bread. They're good plain or with may-onnaise, lettuce, or sprouts. Avocado Dip (p. 69) makes a special pita filling to serve at a party (see picture of pita filling on page 69).

MOCK SALMON SPREAD

A participant in on of our classes, who has always been a lover of smoked salmon, said if his eyes were closed he could easily be fooled into thinking he was eating his old favorite.

> 2 cups raw almonds
> 1 cup raw carrot pieces
> ½ to ¾ cup carrot juice or water
> 1 tablespoon lemon juice
> 1½ celery stalks, cut in pieces
> 4 green onions, chopped or 2 tablespoons dried chives
> 1 teaspoon each salt and paprika
> 1 or 2 tablespoons Wright's Hickory Seasoning or other hickory-smoked seasoning (optional)

1. Place almonds, water, lemon juice, and ½ cup of carrot pieces in blender (or food processor). Blend into a puree.

2. Add remaining ingredients and blend briefly, enough to grind the carrots and celery into a spreadable consistency. Add chives last and blend a few seconds to mix. Refrigerate until ready to serve. Good on crackers or in sandwiches.

❧*Makes 2½ cups.*

ALMOND-OLIVE SPREAD

When my girls were still children, we needed something in a hurry to put on bread, so I blended raw almonds, adding some green ripe olives. It has been a favorite ever since, and never fails to get compliments wherever I serve it. Especially good on rye bread or Rye Krisp.

> 1 cup raw almonds
> 1 cup water
> 1 cup pitted olives (may use green ripe or black)
> ½ teaspoon salt (or more to taste)
> 2 teaspoons onion powder
> ½ teaspoon garlic powder

1. Blend almonds and water until smooth, adding seasonings and a bit more water if needed to keep the almonds blending into a thick cream.

2. Add olives and blend briefly (or longer, depending on how finely blended you like the olives).

Don't yield to the temptation to use a whole can of olives—it's too much!

Serve on crackers or bread.

❧*Makes 2 cups.*

Broiled Open-face

These presentations are especially nice when serving guests—your family will love them too! Any of these open-face sandwiches are made better by placing on a cookie sheet on the top rack of the oven. Turn broiler on high. Leave for 2 to 3 minutes or until beginning to brown on the edges. If you toast the bread in your toaster before spreading, the sandwich will be more crisp on the bottom.

Spread whole wheat french bread with **Simple Butter (p. 56)** and sprinkle with garlic salt.

French bread with **Spinach Filling (p. 67)**

Welsh rarebit-style on English muffin or bread. Spread bread with mayonnaise, add a tomato slice, and top with **Simple Cheese Sauce (p. 26)**.

SWEET PEPPER AND CHEESE MELTS

¼ cup finely diced green and red peppers

½ cup **Ranch-style Dressing (p. 57)** or **Simple Mayonnaise (p. 57)**

1 cup yellow or white (or both) shredded **Sliceable Cashew Cheese (p. 73)** (or purchased shredded vegan cheese)

4 or 5 cherry or roma tomato slices

1 loaf sliced whole wheat french bread

Mix together dressing or mayonnaise and peppers. Spread on each slice of french bread. Sprinkle on a layer of shredded cheese. Broil until edges are lightly toasted.

Toasted Cheese Melt

Same as Sweet Pepper Melt, but omit mayonnaise or dressing, and just place cheese on bread or toast and broil.

Cheeseburger Melt

Spread a half burger bun with mayonnaise. Add an onion and tomato slice, an Oat Burger patty (p. 35), and top with Simple Cheese Sauce (p. 26). Place a toothpick through the center to hold together. Broil. Garnish by placing a pitted olive over the toothpick.

SPINACH DIP

This is our version of the time-honored recipe found on a Knorr Onion Dip package.

1 cup firm tofu or 12-ounce box tofu

⅓ cup raw cashew nuts (optional)

1 tablespoon lemon juice

1 tablespoon honey or sugar

1 tablespoon **Chicken-Like Seasoning**

1 tablespoon onion powder

½ teaspoon garlic powder

1-2 teaspoons salt

water as needed

1 tablespoon potato flour (optional)

½ red bell pepper, chopped

1 can water chestnuts, chopped

10-ounce package thoroughly drained, chopped spinach

1. Blend first eight ingredients until smooth, adding only enough water for all the mixture to go through the blades easily. Add potato flour if too runny and blend for 1 minute.

2. Pour into a mixing bowl and add remaining ingredients. Chill 2-3 hours. Use as a dip or cracker spread, or filling for **Stuffed Italian Bread (p. 66)**

Makes 4 cups.

SLICEABLE CASHEW CHEESE

This recipe doubles for two kinds of cheeselike slices—yellow or white. They can even be shredded!

2 cups water

3 tablespoons agar flakes (or 3 teaspoons agar powder)

1 cup raw cashew nuts

2 tablespoons pimentos or ½ red bell pepper

1 tablespoon lemon juice

1 tablespoon food yeast flakes

1½ teaspoons salt

½ teaspoon onion powder

¼ teaspoon garlic powder

1. **Boil together the agar and water for 1-2 minutes. Place in blender with all the remaining ingredients and blend for 1 or 2 minutes until very smooth.**

2. **Pour into containers and chill. Slice when firm.**

Hint: This recipe makes a yellow cheese. Leave out the pimentos for white cheese. It may be frozen—shreds best when partially frozen. Makes a great topping for pizza or lasagna because it melts when heated. Keep white and yellow cheese (whole and shredded) on hand in the freezer—for quick, nice-looking toasted cheese melts.

Makes 2 cups.

CREAM CHEESE SPREAD

1 can coconut milk

1 cup raw cashew nuts

1 tablespoon food yeast flakes

1 tablespoon lemon juice

1 teaspoon honey or ½ tablespoon sugar

1½ teaspoons salt

Place in blender and blend for at least 1 minute until smooth. Bring to a boil on stove, stirring constantly. Pour into containers, cover, and chill to thicken.

Hint: Divide into smaller amounts and make several flavors before chilling.

Variations: *add to ½ cup spread:*
Strawberry: *2 tablespoons sugar-free strawberry jam.*

French Onion Spread: *1 tablespoon dried onion flakes, 1 teaspoon onion powder, ¼ teaspoon garlic powder, and 1 teaspoon Beef-Like Seasoning.*

Dill and Chive Spread: *¼ teaspoon dill weed, 2 teaspoons chopped fresh or dried chives, 1 teaspoon onion powder, and ⅛ teaspoon garlic powder.*

Pimento Cheese Spread: *Blend into 1 cup Cream Cheese Spread, ¼ cup pimentos, 1 teaspoon onion powder, and ¼ teaspoon garlic powder.*

DELI SANDWICHES

Inspired by those big meal-in-one sandwiches we made every day for our customers at Five Loaves Deli and Bakery.

❧Garden Sandwich
Whole wheat or rye bread with mayonnaise, sliced avocado, alfalfa sprouts, leaf lettuce, and toasted sunflower seeds

❧Lunch Meat Bagel or Hoagie
Unsliced whole wheat bagels can be sliced in thirds: toast the middle section for breakfast, and use the top and bottom for a traveling sandwich that won't get soggy. Use Veggie Cutlet slices (p. 37), pickle, lettuce, and mayonnaise.

❧ "Cheese" sandwich
Sliceable Cashew Cheese (p. 73) or sliced Chedda Polenta (p. 66) with mayonnaise, lettuce, and pickle

SANDWICH FILLINGS

❧Cutlet Salad Filling
1 cup Veggie Cutlet chunks (p. 37)

¼ cup Simple Mayonnaise (p. 57)

½ cup diced celery or chopped water chestnuts

¼ cup chopped green or red pepper

¼ cup diced pickle

Coarsely grind cutlets in food processor. Mix with remaining ingredients.

❧*Makes 2 cups.*

❧Garbanzo-Carrot Filling
2 cups canned or cooked garbanzos

1 medium carrot, shredded

½ cup diced celery

⅓ cup peanut butter

1½ teaspoon onion powder

½ teaspoon dill weed

¼ cup diced pickles

½ teaspoon salt

¼ cup finely diced red or green pepper

½ cup Simple Mayonnaise (p. 57)

Mash the garbanzos and stir in the remaining ingredients. Mix well, adding more or less Simple Mayonnaise to the desired consistency.

❧*Makes 4 cups (use half recipe for small family—keeps only 3 days).*

VEGETABLE WRAPS

4-5 large flour tortillas, whole wheat or white

⅓ cup Simple Mayonnaise or Ranch-style Dressing (p. 57)

1 recipe Roasted Vegetable Filling (p. 45)

1. Place tortillas in a plastic bag and warm in the microwave for about 40 seconds, until just warm (not too long or they will become tough). Or place one at a time on a preheated nonstick skillet over medium-high heat for about 30 seconds. Stack and cover with a cloth or place in a plastic bag to keep moist and warm.

Note: If you don't warm the tortillas, they will be stiff and brittle, and likely to crack when rolled.

2. Spread a tablespoon of mayonnaise or dressing down the center of each tortilla and about ½ cup of vegetable filling (and lettuce if desired). Turn up the bottom to make a small fold, then roll the sides toward the middle—the bottom folded in and the top open.

3. Place in 8-inch casserole or on plate, cover with a cloth, and keep warm in a 175°F oven until ready to serve. Or chill and serve cool. Great food for a sack lunch, picnic, or hike!

EGGLIKE SALAD SANDWICH

Creamy, tangy, and crunchy—just the right combination to put in a sandwich or serve as a salad.

8 ounces firm tofu, crumbled

⅓ cup **Simple Mayonnaise** (p. 57) or other

¼ cup green and red pepper, diced

¼ cup sliced celery

¼ cup diced pickle

2 teaspoons Chicken-Like Seasoning or ½ teaspoon curry powder and 1 teaspoon salt

Mix all ingredients together. Cover, and chill till serving time (2-24 hours).

To serve, spread the tofu mixture on lettuce-lined toast. Also delicious as a filling between two slices of whole grain bread or in pocket bread.

🌿*Makes 2 cups.*

Fruit Variation *(pictured below): Omit green and red peppers and pickles and replace them with the same quantities of green seedless grapes, golden raisins, and toasted slivered almonds.*

Quick and junky snack foods are a constant temptation in our busy lives. Here are a few suggestions for foods to keep on hand to help you survive on the road, or to take on a flight—or even better, to take on a summertime hike!

Healthy Snacks

Crunchy Cluster

GRANOLA BARS

1 cup brown rice syrup or corn syrup

⅓ cup honey

2 teaspoons vanilla

1 teaspoon coconut extract

3 tablespoons peanut butter

4 cups granola

4 cups puffed rice or Rice Krispies cereal

½ cup each: sesame, pumpkin, and sunflower seeds

½ cup unsweetened, flaked coconut

1 cup dry-roasted peanuts

1½ cup raisins or dried cranberries

1. Place first four ingredients in a 2-quart kettle and simmer for 10 minutes. (Don't use a smaller pot—it will boil over!) Remove from heat and stir in peanut butter.

2. Combine all remaining ingredients in a large bowl and add hot syrup mixture. Mix to coat evenly.

3. Spread onto a Bake Magic-lined (or oiled) 12" x 17" sheet pan that has sides. Press lightly in place with wet hands.

4. Bake at 350°F for 10-15 minutes or until bars begin to brown on the edges. Remove and cool for 20 minutes and then, with an oiled knife, cut into squares while still slightly soft.

5. When cool, store in plastic bags, not an airtight container, or they will soften.

➤Makes about 24 bars.

COCONUT BARS

1½ cups unsweetened coconut

1½ cups Brazil nuts or walnuts

2 cups whole wheat pastry flour

1 cup quick oats

1 teaspoon salt

½ cup date pieces

2 tablespoons honey

1 cup water

1 teaspoon vanilla

1. Place coconut, Brazil nuts, and flour in a food processor and blend for 1 minute. Put in a mixing bowl–add oats and salt.

2. Blend dates, honey, and water until smooth and add to the nut and flour mixture with salt and vanilla. Stir together and then mix with hands, adding a little more water as needed to make a dough that is moist but not sticky.

3. Use nonstick or Bake Magic-lined 12" x 17" sheet pan and cover with plastic wrap. Roll flat with a rolling pin to about ¼ inch thick. Score with a knife into rectangles or diamonds before baking.

4. Bake at 350°F for 20-25 minutes.

➤Makes about 50 bars.

FIBER BARS

These tasty bars are great for traveling. My friend Leslie Caza gave me this recipe. Teenagers love to grab them as they run out the door.

1 cup dry-roasted peanuts

½ cup sunflower seeds

½ cup walnuts

¼ cup carob powder (optional)

1 cup granola (or ¾ cup Grape Nuts)

1 cup flaxseed meal

2 cups Rice Krispies or equivalent crushed rice cakes

½ teaspoon salt

½ cup honey

1 tablespoon vanilla

¼ cup water

1. Place peanuts, sunflower seeds, walnuts, and carob powder in a food processor and blend with the steel blade for 1 minute, or until a fine powder. Add the granola (or Grape-Nuts) and blend briefly to make a coarse meal.

2. Place nut mixture in a mixing bowl and stir in flaxseed meal and the Rice Krispies. Add the honey, vanilla, and water. Mix well with hands.

3. Press into a 9" x 9" baking pan that has been lightly oiled. Score/cut into 16 squares. Bake 15 minutes at 350°F.

It might seem like too much mix for the pan, but they will press in and be about 1 inch thick when finished.

DRIED BANANAS

This wonderful travel food was first introduced to us years ago by some camping friends . We tried some, not expecting to like them. A few bites, and we were hooked. They are especially good eaten with almonds!

1. Buy ripe bananas on sale. They are best for drying when they are speckled.

Don't try to dry them when green or even partly green—they will be tasteless and brittle.

2. Split the bananas in thirds by gently forcing your finger into the bottom of the peeled banana toward the top. As your finger slides up the core of the banana, it will separate in three long strips.

3. Place banana strips on a screen and leave in a food dehydrator for about 8-12 hours. When finished, they won't feel soft in the center, but should be pliable (not crisp). Place in plastic bags and store in a refrigerator or freezer.

Tip: A food dehydrator is a nice device for drying fruits, vegetables, and other foods for backpacking. Small ones are not expensive to buy, and if you watch, you will probably be able to find one in a thrift store for very little. Meanwhile, you can try making dried bananas in your oven. Place them on a cooling rack in the oven at the lowest setting overnight—crack the door open for circulation air.

ROASTED ALMONDS

Compare the value of good whole almonds to Cheetos or chips. We always bring almonds when traveling. My husband likes them raw, and I like them roasted. They are delicious eaten with dried fruit. Better than an Almond Joy!

2 tablespoons water

1 teaspoon salt

4 cups raw almonds

1. Place water and salt in a mixing bowl, and stir together until salt is dissolved.

2. Add the almonds and mix until all the nuts are coated.

3. Place almonds on a cookie sheet and bake at 250°F for about 2 hours. Check occasionally for doneness by cutting a nut in half. When it is light brown inside, it is time to take the nuts out.

TOASTED PUMPKIN SEEDS

My mother used to make these, and we all loved them. (And so did our frequent guests.) Using the microwave makes them puff up into little round, crunchy bullets. You can toast them in the oven, like the almonds above, but they won't puff as much.

2 tablespoons water

¾ teaspoon salt

1 teaspoon onion powder

¼ or ½ teaspoon garlic powder

4 cups raw pumpkin seeds

1. Mix together the water and seasonings in a mixing bowl.

2. Add the pumpkin seeds and stir until coated.

3. Place in a microwave container with lid. Cook in microwave on high for 4 minutes. Stir, cover, and return for 2 more minutes. Stir. Return for 2 more minutes, depending on your microwave. They will puff up and brown when done. Remove and pour out onto a tray to cool.

RICE CHEX SNACKS

Most people like something crunchy and salty to round out a meal on the road. Most recipes for this snack call for butter or margarine. We served this fat-free version at an evening social occasion where a light refreshment was needed. Our guests cleaned up the bowl, and I was rewarded with a new recipe for "something better" than potato chips.

Honey Sesame Flavor

2 tablespoons honey

2 tablespoons coconut milk

½ tablespoon **Chicken-Like Seasoning**

1 teaspoon onion powder

½ teaspoon salt

4 cups Rice or Corn Chex

1 cups pretzel sticks

½ cup each slivered almonds, sesame seeds

Barbecue Flavor

2 tablespoons honey

2 tablespoons water

1 teaspoon molasses

1 tablespoon peanut butter

1 teaspoon **Wright's Hickory Seasoning**

1 teaspoon paprika

1 teaspoon salt

1 teaspoon lemon juice

4 cups Rice or Corn Chex Cereal

1 cup pretzel sticks

1 cup pumpkin seeds or peanuts

1. Mix together the honey, milk or water, and flavorings in a large mixing bowl. Add the rest and stir until all are coated.

2. Pour onto a cookie sheet and bake at 250°F for about 1½ hours. Stir and gently break up clumps with your hands once or twice during baking.

Makes 4 cups.

SURVIVAL COOKIES

I always bring cookies on a trip. They keep well, are easy to bag up and store, and take little space. Stick several in your purse when traveling on the airlines—you almost always need them. Check the ingredients for Peanut Butter 'n' Honey Cookies (p. 90)—they're the same as eating a peanut butter and honey sandwich.

BACKPACK SANDWICHES

Do you need fresh ideas for a sandwich to put in a sack or backpack? Try Vegetable Wraps (p. 75) or Bagel Sandwiches (p. 74). We like them because in addition to giving a change, they can't be smashed.

Dessert Secrets

Never underestimate the power of a tempting dessert to make everyone happy now and sick later! But now you can offer your family sweet endings to their meals without bringing on the colds or adding to their waistlines.

These desserts are a wonderful explosion of taste, yet they will actually lower your cholesterol. This is true because they are made with fiber-rich grains (such as oatmeal), healthy fats (such as Brazil nuts), and options for natural sweeteners (such as honey and dates). When you taste these desserts, you will hardly be able to believe the calorie count. Partake with moderation, of course, and you can enjoy them guilt-free.

CAKES

With the basic principles you have learned this far, you will now see how easy it is to make desserts the natural way. Let's start with a basic cake recipe.

First, a few tips:

Flour: Bread flour has a higher gluten content and gives this cake a slightly better texture, but unbleached or pastry flour can be used.

Sweeteners: In making these recipes over and over, we have learned which sweeteners work best. That will be listed in the ingredients first. But options are given for you to choose. Sugar generally works better in the cakes, but you can use the less-refined products such as natural cane juice or *Sucanat* (which is less sweet, so you will need to use more). If you use honey, warm it so it is runny, and substitute it for that amount of water or other liquid in the recipe. Pick what is best for you, and use less if your family can enjoy not-so-sweet cake.

If you're struggling to make this all work and don't have a substitute, you can use regular sugar. Use it more sparingly—you'll notice that these desserts are not as sweet as in most books. So even if you use table sugar, it will be less than normal, and your family will likely be satisfied anyway. But when you settle into the new way of doing things, make the transition from sugar to something a little better!

Baking Powder: We use *Ener-G Baking Powder* because it is free of aluminum and other chemicals that are irritating. It can be ordered by mail (see Appendix). Other options for baking powder are given in the recipes.

Storing: After the cake has cooled 5-10 minutes in the pan, remove and wrap the warm cake loosely in plastic wrap (not too tight, or as it cools your cake will compress). This keeps the cake moist, and oil-free cakes need more protection from drying out. Then place the wrapped cake in a plastic bag if you want to freeze it. Frozen cake is easier to frost with **Whipped Topping** (p. 99) icing.

CREATE-a-CAKE

What's your favorite cake? Carrot, applesauce, banana, mango, persimmon, pumpkin? Use this recipe and have some fun. The same recipe also makes muffins, cupcakes or banana bread.

Dry ingredients
¾ cup whole wheat and ½ cup unbleached white flour

¾ teaspoon salt

Choose a baking powder
1 tablespoon Ener-G

2 teaspoons Rumford

½ tablespoon Calumet or other

Wet ingredients
½ cup coconut milk or Cashew Cream (p. 107) or soy milk

1 teaspoon vanilla

water as needed

Choose a sweetener
⅓ cup fructose

or ⅓ cup honey, warmed (omit water)

or ½ cup sugar or natural cane juice

or ¾ cup Sucanat

Choose one (omit for plain cake)
⅓ cup applesauce, or crushed pineapple, or pumpkin

⅓ cup mashed ripe banana, or mango, or persimmon

½ cup finely grated carrots plus 2 tablespoons water

Extras (add to dry ingredients)
1 cup raisins

⅓ cup chopped nuts

1 teaspoon coriander or other spice

⅜ cup ground flaxseed (decrease flour by ¼ cup) (gives the cake a spongier texture, but makes it darker)

1. Preheat oven to 400°F. Prepare cake pan (8-inch square or round) by coating with a light mist of oil. Use of baking parchment makes it easy to remove cake. Cut to fit; oil sides of pan. Make cupcakes if desired. Spray-paper cupcake cups lightly with oil.

2. Combine flour, baking powder, salt, and sugar (unless you use honey) in a bowl. Add raisins, nuts, or ground flax if desired.

3. Combine milk, honey, and vanilla in a measuring cup. Stir in fruit or carrots. Add water if needed to equal 1 cup of liquid. Stir wet ingredients into the dry mix until well mixed.

Because ingredients are variable, evaluate the consistency at this point, adding a bit more flour or water to make a soft batter that holds its shape. It should be about the consistency of soft ice cream. If it is too stiff, the cake will not rise as well, and will look rough on top when baked. Too wet a mix will cause the cake to rise and fall slightly, making the top either flat or caved-in. Experience will teach you how it should look.

4. Bake at 400°F for 5 minutes. Reduce heat to 350°F and bake for 20-25 minutes, until knife inserted in center comes out clean and edges of cake are beginning to pull away from sides of pan.

5. Let cool in pan 10 minutes. Then remove from pan and wrap loosely with plastic wrap while warm.

6. If desired, after cake has cooled 10 minutes, put it on a plate and spread with Maple Nut Glaze (below) or Carob Frosting (p. 81). Let cool 1 hour before slipping it, plate and all, into a plastic bag (or freeze and top with Whipped Topping [p. 99]).

MAPLE NUT GLAZE

½ cup pure maple syrup (or ½ cup honey and 1 teaspoon maple flavoring)

½ teaspoon agar powder (or ½ tablespoon agar flakes)

½ teaspoon butter-flavored salt (or plain)

¼ cup soy milk

½ cup chopped walnuts

1. Place all ingredients (except walnuts) in a saucepan. Bring to a boil, reduce heat, and simmer 3 minutes, stirring occasionally.

2. Set aside at room temperature until semi-set (about 10 minutes). Spread glaze on cake and sprinkle with chopped walnuts.

"Tufts University researchers interviewed more than 900 men and women aged 69 to 93 about their diets and measured their bone mineral density at several skeletal sites."
"Men who consumed the most fruit, vegetables, and cereal had denser bones, and women who ate a great deal of candy had the lowest bone mineral density."

American Journal of Clinical Nutrition 76 (2002): 245-252

"The mind does not wear out nor break down so often on account of diligent employment and hard study, as on account of eating improper food at improper times, and of careless inattention to the laws of health. ...Diligent study is not the principal cause of the breaking down of the mental powers. The main cause is improper diet, irregular meals, and a lack of physical exercise. Irregular hours for eating and sleeping sap the brain forces."

E. G. White, Counsels on Diet and Foods, pp. 122, 123

FLUFFY SHORTCAKE OR SCONES

1. Make Coffee Cake dough (p. 23).

2. Scoop shortcakes onto two lightly oiled cookie sheets with a medium ice-cream scoop. Rap cookie sheet briskly on the counter three or four times to flatten cakes into large, cookie-shaped circles. Or bake in a loaf pan and slice like pound cake.

3. Bake at 350°F for 15 minutes. Shortcakes are done when golden brown underneath.

4. Serve shortcake with mashed strawberries or raspberries sweetened with honey and apple juice concentrate. Top with ice cream or Whipped Topping (p. 99) (see picture on page 84). For scones, split and serve with jam.

❧Makes 10 to 12.

ORANGE CAKE

Delicious example of Create-a-Cake recipe! It uses a little extra sweetener because of the tart orange.

½ cup whole wheat bread flour

¾ cup unbleached white flour*

½ cup sugar

1 tablespoon Ener-G Baking Powder (or ½ tablespoon regular)

¾ teaspoon salt

½ cup coconut milk

⅛ cup frozen orange juice concentrate

¼ large orange with half the peel removed

¼ cup water, approximately

White flour is used in this recipe to make a prettier cake. If you don't mind a darker color, go ahead and use all whole wheat. I grind my own flour and use white whole wheat—it is a very light color and nice for cakes.

1. Preheat oven to 400°F. Place flours, sugar, baking powder, and salt in a mixing bowl and mix together.

2. Blend together the remaining ingredients, adding enough water to equal 1¼ cups total liquid in the blender.

3. Mix the liquid into the dry ingredients in the mixing bowl. Stir briskly, or use an electric hand mixer and beat for about 20 seconds. Immediately pour into an 8-inch round or square baking pan.

4. Place cake in 400°F oven for 5 minutes, then reduce temperature to 350°F for about 20 minutes, or until knife inserted in center of cake comes out clean and cake is beginning to lightly brown and pull away from the sides.

5. Remove cake from oven and cool for about 10 minutes in the pan, then cover the pan and cake with plastic wrap or place it in a plastic bag to keep it moist until served.

ORANGE LAYER CAKE

Orange Cake pictured is a layered cake but can be made as single layer if desired.

You can double the recipe and divide batter into two or three 8-inch cake pans.* It's helpful to line the pans with baking parchment for easy removal when cakes are finished. Let them sit for about 5 minutes after removing from the oven,

then remove them to a wire rack and wrap each one loosely, while still hot, with plastic wrap (keeps it moist). Place in a plastic bag and freeze. (Frozen cakes are easier to decorate with frosting!) When ready to decorate, remove from freezer and stack with Pineapple-Orange Filling (below) between layers. Spread top and sides with Whipped Topping (p. 99). Some of the icing may be colored with a drop or two of food coloring and used in a pastry tube for decorating.

Tip: A double recipe also fits a 9" x 13" cake pan.

PINEAPPLE-ORANGE FILLING

2 cups crushed pineapple

½ cup frozen orange juice concentrate

¼ cup honey

⅛ teaspoon lemon extract

2 tablespoons cornstarch dissolved in ¼ cup water

Place all ingredients (except cornstarch) in a saucepan. Bring to a boil and slowly add dissolved cornstarch, stirring constantly until thick. Cool for easier spreading between layers.

BANANA BREAD

Note: this is a variation of the Create-a-Cake recipe.

1 cup whole wheat flour

½ cup unbleached flour

¾ teaspoon salt

1 tablespoon Ener-G Baking Powder

⅓ cup chopped walnuts

½ cup coconut milk or Cashew Cream (p. 107)

⅓ cup honey (or ½ cup sugar and 2 tablespoons water)

½ cup mashed ripe banana

1. Mix dry ingredients in a medium-sized bowl. Add walnuts.

2. Mix remaining ingredients in a 2-cup measuring cup and add water if needed to equal 1 cup of liquid.

3. Briskly stir liquid into dry ingredients, and pour into an oiled loaf pan. Bake at 350°F for about 40-45 minutes, or until knife inserted in center comes out clean.

☙*Makes 1 loaf.*

CAROB CAKE OR BROWNIES

Before I was married, my experience in the kitchen was pretty elementary—making macaroni and cheese with a Kraft mix or making brownies with a Betty Crocker mix. Here's a "graduate level" brownie recipe. You'll have to pull out a few more ingredients from the pantry, but the cells in your body will know what to do with everything, and your taste buds will be just as happy. Notice the flaxseeds—good for your cholesterol and for making baked goods lighter!

1½ cups whole wheat flour

1 tablespoon Ener-G Baking Powder

¾ teaspoon salt

1 cup coconut milk

⅔ cup brown or raw sugar

1 teaspoon vanilla

1 teaspoon Roma coffee substitute

¼ cup carob powder

¼ cup flaxseeds

⅓ cup applesauce

1. Combine flour, baking powder, and salt in a mixing bowl.

2. Place remaining ingredients in blender and blend until smooth.

3. Pour blended mix into flour mixture and stir together until well mixed.

4. Pour into a lightly oiled 8-inch square pan. Bake at 350°F for 30 minutes.

☙*Makes 16 squares or 12 cupcakes.*

CAROB FROSTING

¼ cup dry-roasted peanuts

3 tablespoons carob powder

½ cup water

¼ cup maple syrup

¼ cup brown sugar

½ teaspoon salt

½ teaspoon agar powder

1. Blend until smooth and bring to a boil. Simmer 3 minutes.

2. Remove from heat and set aside at room temperature until semi-set (about 20 minutes).

3. Spread frosting over cake and sprinkle with toasted walnuts if desired.

PIES AND CRUSTS

My husband's German mother specialized in making delicious desserts. Her "secret" to make a tender, flaky piecrust was to add an extra-heaping tablespoon of shortening! Now I apply the same principle in making a natural crust without oil or shortening. We use enough unrefined fat to keep the crust from being tough, and people usually enjoy every wholesome bite. Besides, it's much easier to make and roll out, using two pieces of plastic. See the simple directions, and you'll be an expert at making piecrust.

SIMPLE AND FLAKY PIECRUST

Crust pictured left with Dutch Apple Pie filling (p. 84).

- ½ cup flour (barley, whole wheat pastry, or unbleached white)
- ⅔ cup Brazil nuts*
- ¾ teaspoon salt
- ½ cup quick oats
- ¼ cup or more water

*Other nuts such as almonds, cashews, walnuts, or even coconut may be used, but if using a nut that has a lower fat content (such as almonds or cashews), increase amount to 1 cup and decrease flour by 2 tablespoons. If you don't have a food processor, you can make this crust with purchased nut butter, such as almond butter. Use ⅓ cup and work it into the flour with your hands, then add the water.

1. Place flour, nuts, and salt in a food processor and blend about 1 minute, until nuts are ground as fine as the flour.

2. Remove to a mixing bowl and stir in the oats. Add water, gently forming dough into a ball with your hands. Add a bit more water, if needed, for a soft but not sticky ball of dough.

3. Roll the dough from center to edges, forming a 12-inch circle.

Hint: This is most easily done by rolling between two pieces of plastic bag material. Remove the top piece of plastic and invert the pie plate over the rolled-out dough. Slip hand under the bottom plastic with pie dough and plate on top. Quickly flip it over so the dough is now over the plate, and peel off the plastic. Gently shape the dough into the plate with fingers, patching where necessary. This dough is very workable and patches well.

4. Trim pastry to ½ inch beyond edge of plate. Fold under extra pastry and crimp edge.

5. For a prebaked crust, prick bottom and sides of pastry generously with the tines of a fork. Prick where bottom and sides meet all around the pie shell.

Bake at 400°F for 10-12 minutes or until golden.

6. For a double crust pie, make 1½ times the recipe and fill unbaked pastry with your choice of fruit filling. Add top crust, slit in several places and bake until done.

CRUMBLE NUT CRUST

This is Kimberley's recipe, and it has become our favorite graham-cracker-like crust.

- ½ cup unsweetened coconut
- ½ cup raw almonds
- ⅔ cup flour (whole wheat pastry or barley) or ¾ cup quick oats
- ½ teaspoon salt
- 2 tablespoons honey (warm and runny)(may use 2 tablespoons sugar and 2 or 3 tablespoons water)

1. Place coconut, almonds, flour, and salt in food processor. Blend together for about 30 seconds. Then add honey and blend about 15 seconds. Turn off processor and test mixture with your fingers. If it seems too dry and crumbly, add a bit more honey—just enough to feel soft and moist. It should stick together slightly when pressed. But be careful not to get it too wet, or it will not be as tender and light when baked.

2. Press into a lightly oiled pie plate, shaping with fingers to make a nicely formed piecrust. It helps to put a piece of plastic wrap over the crust or put your hand in a small plastic bag while pressing the crust. This keeps the mixture from sticking to your fingers as you work.

3. Bake at 375°F for about 10 minutes.

Variation: *Coconut-Oat Crust*
Use ¾ cup quick oats and ¾ cup coconut, following above instructions.

Strawberry Cream Pie

Pear-Plum Crisp

Dutch Apple Pie

Fluffy Shortcake

Dutch Apple Pie

Do you remember the wonderful smell of an apple pie baking in the oven when you came home from school? This pie also fills the house with the aroma of toasted nuts and coconut—an experience that will make homecoming a top priority to your family. The coconut in this crust makes it light—in both color and texture.

Filling:

6 cups sliced cooking apples

1 rounded teaspoon coriander

½ teaspoon ginger (optional)

½ teaspoon salt

1 teaspoon vanilla

¼ cup apple juice concentrate

¼ cup pure maple syrup or honey

2 tablespoons fructose (optional) (may need more if some apples are tart)

3 tablespoons cornstarch dissolved in ¼ cup water

Crust:

½ cup quick oats

½ cup whole wheat pastry or unbleached white flour

1 cup raw almonds

½ cup unsweetened coconut

1 teaspoon salt

⅓ cup water

½ cup quick oats

2 tablespoons honey, warmed

1. Make apple filling by placing all in a kettle except the dissolved cornstarch.

Bring to a boil, cover, and simmer for 10 minutes, until apples begin to soften.

2. While apples are simmering, make crust by placing oats, flour, almonds, coconut, and salt in food processor. Blend with the steel blade for about 1½ minutes until fine. Add water and whiz briefly to mix.

3. Remove half the dough from food processor and form into a ball with hands.

4. Place ball of dough between two sheets of plastic (see Simple and Flaky Piecrust instructions [p. 83]), and roll into a circle to fit a 9-inch pie plate. Trim pastry to edge of plate and flute edges.

5. When apples have simmered for 10 minutes, slowly stir in the dissolved cornstarch. Place hot filling in the unbaked piecrust.

6. Add oats and honey to the rest of the dough in the food processor, and whiz a few seconds, just to mix together. Sprinkle crumb topping over the top, and bake at 350°F for about 40 minutes until crust and topping are golden brown and filling is bubbling at the edges of the pie.

Check after it has baked 25 minutes and cover loosely with foil for the last 15 minutes to keep from getting too brown.

Variations:

Double Crust Pie: Instead of adding oats and honey to remainder of dough in food processor, roll it out and place on top of the pie. Press edges together and flute. Slit top crust to let steam escape as it bakes.

Cranberry-Apple: Add ½ cup fresh or frozen cranberries to the apple filling after it has been thickened with cornstarch.

Peach-Plum: Use 4 cups sliced fresh or frozen peaches and 2 cups sliced purple plums. Good with white grape juice concentrate instead of apple juice, and honey instead of maple syrup. This pie is more juicy than apple pie. Dissolve and add more cornstarch until filling is as thick as jam, so when it cools it will keep its shape when sliced.

Three-Berry Pie: Follow Peach-Plum directions, replacing peaches and plums with 2 cups each blueberries, boysenberries, strawberries, or raspberries.

STRAWBERRY CREAM PIE

The filling for this Strawberry Cream Pie is a basic recipe that is loaded with possibilities. It's called Cashew Cheese Cake in Best Gourmet Recipes, but we think you will like this new twist. Then you will want to think of other ways to use this idea! See picture on page 83.

Cream Filling:
⅔ cup water

1 teaspoon agar powder (1 tablespoon flakes)

½ cup cashew nuts

¼ cup honey

½ cup pineapple juice

½ teaspoon salt

water to equal 2 cups total mixture

1. Make and bake a Crumble Nut Crust (p. 83).

2. Place water and agar in a saucepan and bring to a boil. Reduce heat and simmer for 1-2 minutes.

3. Place agar mixture in blender along with remaining ingredients, except extra water. Blend for about 2 minutes until smooth. Turn off blender and add water to equal 2 cups total mixture. Blend briefly to mix.

4. Pour into baked 9-inch Crumble Nut Crust and place in refrigerator for 1 hour.

After it sets up, make the surface rough by scoring with a fork (or topping will slide when served).

Strawberry Topping and Glaze:
¾ cup Welch's White Grape Raspberry Concentrate

2 tablespoons each honey, and water

½ teaspoon agar powder (½ tablespoon flakes)

1½ cups fresh strawberries, cut in half lengthwise

Boil juice, honey and agar together 1-2 minutes. Cool 10 minutes in refrigerator. Slice the strawberries and arrange them on the pie. The glaze should start to thicken a bit, but don't let it set up. Pour the glaze over the strawberries on the pie. Chill until glaze sets up.

To fill a 9" x 13" pan, double the glaze and crumble crust, triple the cream filling, and use 1 pint strawberries.

FRESH PEACH CREAM PIE

Instead of strawberries, use sliced peaches. For the glaze, use white grape juice concentrate instead of raspberry juice.

BLUEBERRY CREAM DESSERT

Make a double recipe of Strawberry Cream Pie filling (above) and pour into an 8-inch square pan that has a baked Crumble Nut Crust (p. 83) on the bottom. Or just cover bottom with a thin layer of Grape Nuts cereal or granola crumbs and gently pour blended filling over crumbs. Chill 3 or 4 hours and serve with a blueberry topping (see Fresh Fruit Sauce [p. 19]).

OLD-FASHIONED BAKED PUMPKIN PIE

This is one of the easiest pies to make, and is just as foolproof as one made with milk and eggs. You will notice the absence of the usual cinnamon or pumpkin-pie spice. That is because we avoid the use of irritating spices. I think you will find the sweet, rich flavor of pumpkin with the delicate blend of maple and coriander delightful, and the spices won't be missed.

1¾ cups cooked pumpkin (15-ounce can)

1 can coconut milk

½ cup pitted dates

½ cup honey

¼ cup cornstarch

1 teaspoon vanilla

½ teaspoon maple flavoring

½ teaspoon coriander

½ teaspoon salt

½ teaspoon fresh pealed or dry ginger (optional)

1. Blend all ingredients in the blender until smooth.

2. Pour into an unbaked pie shell and bake at 350°F for 1 hour.

Tip: Here are two lower fat options. Use ½ can coconut milk with ½ can of water or 2 cups soy or nut milk.

FRUIT PIZZA

1. Make ½ recipe Vanilla Custard (p. 97), and pour onto a baked pizza crust (see Cobbler Crust [p. 88]).

2. Chill to set up, and then arrange sliced strawberries, kiwi, mandarin oranges, and raspberries or peaches on top.

3. Slice and serve.

LEMON CREAM PIE

¼ cup cornstarch

½ cup orange juice

1½ cups pineapple juice

1 cup coconut milk (½ can)*

¼ cup honey

2 tablespoons lemon juice

⅛ teaspoon lemon extract

¼ teaspoon salt

1 baked **Crumble Nut Crust** (p. 83)

1. In a medium saucepan, place the cornstarch and ½ cup orange juice. Stir together until dissolved.

2. Add the remaining ingredients and bring to a boil while stirring constantly until thickened.

3. Remove from heat and pour into baked Crumble Nut Crust. Refrigerate several hours to chill. Serve with Whipped Topping (p. 99), if desired.

*Coconut milk can be replaced with ½ cup cashew nuts or 10½-ounce box or ¾-cup soft tofu. If cashews or tofu are used, you will need to use a blender. Add more pineapple juice if needed to make 3¼ cups total mixture.

Variation: *Key Lime*
Instead of lemon juice, use juice and grated peel of one large or two small limes and add about 6 drops of green food coloring.

5. Cover the cobbler loosely with a sheet of plastic or a damp cotton towel. Put in a warm place (on the stove while the oven is heating), and let rise until double, about 45 minutes to an hour.

6. Place raised cobbler in the preheated oven at 350°F and bake for 30 minutes, or until crust is golden brown. Remove from oven and let cool completely before placing in a plastic bag. Refrigerate. To serve, heat uncovered in the oven at 300°F for about 30 minutes. Serve with Five Loaves Rice Cream (p. 99) or Whipped Topping (p. 99).

COBBLER CRUST

This crust is called Basic Pastry Dough in Best Gourmet Recipes. *Here we have cut the size to fit an 8-inch square pan.*

> 1 teaspoon yeast dissolved in 2 tablespoons warm water
>
> ¼ cup coconut milk or Cashew Cream (p. 107)
>
> ½ teaspoon salt
>
> 2 teaspoons sugar
>
> ⅓ cup plus 1 tablespoon whole wheat pastry flour
>
> ⅓ cup unbleached white flour plus a bit more for kneading

1. Place dissolved yeast and coconut milk or Cashew Cream in a mixing bowl. Add the salt, sugar, and whole wheat flour. Stir to mix and then add the white flour, continuing to stir and then to knead with hands into a ball of dough that can be handled.

2. Place dough on a floured surface and knead for 1 or 2 minutes, adding more flour as needed until you have a smooth ball.

3. Roll out the ball into a 9-inch square and place on cobbler as in step 4 above.

Variation: *Pizza Crust*
This crust can also be rolled into a circle for a pizza pan. Let rise and bake. Use for **Fruit Pizza** *(p. 86) or any kind of pizza. It's delicious!*

Tip: Double the recipe to make Calzones *(p. 67) or* Sweet Rolls *(p. 65), or for a 9" x 13" baking dish.*

☙*Makes a 9-inch square cobbler.*

CHERRY COBBLER

In our family, cobbler is synonymous with Grandma. This was her favorite dessert to make—mainly because it was such a good healthful recipe, and she lived in California, where there were lots of fresh fruits to use. Besides cherry, she often made peach or apricot and always had a cobbler or two in her freezer for unexpected company. And she never failed to have homemade ice cream to put on top!

> 4 cups pitted cherries, apricots or peaches (fresh, frozen or canned)
>
> ¾ cup frozen apple juice concentrate
>
> ½ teaspoon almond extract (optional)
>
> ¼ cup honey or sugar if needed
>
> ⅓ cup regular Clear Jel or ¼ cup cornstarch
>
> ½ cup water or juice from fruit

1. Prepare a 9-inch square baking dish by lightly oiling the sides.

2. Place cherries, juice, almond extract, and honey or sugar (if you use it) in a saucepan and bring to a boil.

3. Meanwhile, dissolve the food starch in the water. When the cherries begin to boil, gradually stir in the dissolved starch, adding more or less as needed to make the sauce as thick as pie filling. Remove from heat and pour into a 9-inch square baking pan.

4. Make and roll out the cobbler crust into a 9-inch square. Gently roll the square of dough up onto the rolling pin, and unroll it on top of the hot fruit, adjusting the sides to fit the pan, trimming if necessary. Pierce the dough with a fork or sharp knife in several places to allow the steam to escape while baking.

5. Cover the cobbler loosely with a sheet of plastic or a damp cotton towel. Put in a warm place (on the stove while the oven is heating), and let rise until double, about 45 minutes to an hour.

6. Place raised cobbler in the preheated oven at 350°F and bake for 30 minutes, or until crust is golden brown. Remove from oven and let cool completely before placing in a plastic bag. Refrigerate. To serve, heat uncovered in the oven at 300°F for about 30 minutes. Serve with Five Loaves Rice Cream (p. 99) or Whipped Topping (p. 99).

COBBLER CRUST

This crust is called Basic Pastry Dough in Best Gourmet Recipes. *Here we have cut the size to fit an 8-inch square pan.*

  1 teaspoon yeast dissolved in
    2 tablespoons warm water

¼ cup coconut milk or Cashew Cream (p. 107)

½ teaspoon salt

2 teaspoons sugar

⅓ cup plus 1 tablespoon whole wheat pastry flour

⅓ cup unbleached white flour plus a bit more for kneading

1. Place dissolved yeast and coconut milk or Cashew Cream in a mixing bowl. Add the salt, sugar, and whole wheat flour. Stir to mix and then add the white flour, continuing to stir and then to knead with hands into a ball of dough that can be handled.

2. Place dough on a floured surface and knead for 1 or 2 minutes, adding more flour as needed until you have a smooth ball.

3. Roll out the ball into a 9-inch square and place on cobbler as in step 4 above.

Variation: *Pizza Crust*
This crust can also be rolled into a circle for a pizza pan. Let rise and bake. Use for **Fruit Pizza** *(p. 86) or any kind of pizza. It's delicious!*

Tip: Double the recipe to make Calzones *(p. 67) or* Sweet Rolls *(p. 65), or for a 9" x 13" baking dish.*

✆*Makes a 9-inch square cobbler.*

PEANUT BUTTER 'N' HONEY COOKIES

This is my favorite quick dessert to make. It is loved by all, especially children. The wonderful part of the recipe is its simplicity. We like to take these cookies when traveling, telling ourselves it is the same as eating a peanut butter and honey sandwich.

2 cups dry-roasted peanuts

1 cup whole wheat pastry flour
  or oats

½ cup honey (warmed in microwave)*

1 teaspoon vanilla

1 teaspoon salt (omit if peanuts are
  salted)

*Note: This is a critical step. The honey is the liquid in the recipe. It needs to pour like water or the mix will seem dry and if too much water is added, the cookies will be tough.

1. Place peanuts and flour in a food processor and whiz for about 1 minute until nuts and flour are about the same texture. (Takes about 1 minute. In a Vita-Mix, using the plunger, it takes only about 30 seconds.)

2. Place flour-and-nut mixture in a mixing bowl and add salt. Mix in the honey and vanilla. Stir together and then mix with your hands. (If your food processor is large enough, you can mix the honey and vanilla in the processor. Turn on briefly to mix.)

The dough should hold together without being dry and crumbly. If needed, add a tablespoon of water, but be careful not to get it so wet that it sticks to your hands. It should be like piecrust. If it is too dry, the cookies will crumble and not hold together, but if too wet, they will be hard to handle and the baked cookies will be hard. A little extra flour can be worked in if the dough is too sticky!

3. Pinch off pieces of dough and roll into balls the size of walnuts. Place on a cookie sheet and press flat with hands. Then press flatter with a fork, dipping the fork in water as needed to keep it from sticking to the dough (or use a plastic fork—it won't stick even if dry, but will break unless you press on the tines).

4. Bake at 350°F for about 10 minutes. Watch them carefully. They are done when just beginning to brown on the edges. I can think of nothing that burns so easily as peanut butter cookies. So take them out before it looks like they're done! Let them cool on the cookie sheet before removing.

❧*Makes about 20 cookies.*

Variation: *Gluten-free Cookies Replace whole wheat flour with 1 cup brown rice flour and 2 tablespoons cornstarch.*

Really Good

MOLASSES COOKIES

This variation of the Peanut Butter 'n' Honey Cookie (p. 90) resembles the molasses cookies my grandmother used to make.

- 1 cup walnuts
- 1¾ cups whole wheat pastry flour
- 1 teaspoon salt
- ½ teaspoon ginger (optional)
- ⅓ cup molasses
- ½ cup honey (or ¾ cup brown sugar and ¼ cup water)
- ½ cup applesauce
- 1 teaspoon vanilla
- 1 tablespoon **Ener-G Baking Soda***
- ½ cup pecan or walnut halves (optional)

*Ener-G Baking Powder is not good in cookies because the sour taste of the citric acid remains in the thick dough instead of gassing away in baking, as is the case with cakes and muffins. So I have used calcium carbonate without citric acid (Ener-G—see Glossary) with some success. If you prefer, use 1 teaspoon baking powder or soda.

1. Place nuts, flour, salt, and ginger in food processor and blend for 1 minute until nuts are as fine as the flour.

2. In a mixing bowl, combine flour-and-nut mixture with remaining ingredients. Mix well.

3. Using a small ice-cream scoop, place in mounds on a nonstick or lightly oiled cookie sheet, leaving space between cookies for them to spread out. Rap the cookie sheet sharply on the counter several times (place towel under) to make the cookies spread into larger circles (or flatten with a spatula that has been dipped in water).

4. Bake at 350°F for 15-20 minutes. Let cool on the cookie sheet before serving or storing in an airtight container.

❧*Makes about 20 cookies.*

"High-vegetable fiber intakes reduce risk factors for cardiovascular disease and possibly colon cancer."

Metabolism *50, no. 4 (April 2001): 494-503*

"It is important that the food should be prepared with care, that the appetite, when not perverted, can relish it. Because we from principle discard the use of meat, butter, mince pies, spices, lard, and that which irritates the stomach and destroys health, the idea should never be given that it is of but little consequence what we eat."

E. G. White, Counsels on Health, *p. 151*

FRUIT THINS

1½ cups Brazil nuts or walnuts

1 cup coconut

2 cup quick oats

½ cup whole wheat pastry flour or unbleached white flour

1 teaspoon salt

¼ cup honey, warmed

½ cup water

Filling: use ½ cup water with a, b, or c:

   a: 2 cups raisins, 1 cup dates

   b: 1 cup each dates, raisins, and dried cranberries

   c: 1 cup dried apricots, 1 cup dried pineapple pieces, and 1 cup golden raisins

1. Blend coconut and oatmeal 2 minutes in food processor and place in bowl.

2. Blend nuts, flour, and salt for 30 seconds. Mix in bowl with coconut/oatmeal mixture. Add honey and water and stir together until a pie-dough-like mixture is formed. Divide into two balls.

3. Filling: use a, b, or c from ingredient list; place in food processor with water and whiz, adding extra water if needed to make a thick spreadable paste. *(If dates or dried pineapple are hard, soften with the water in microwave before processing.)*

Tip: Roll the first crust using two large pieces of plastic bag material or Bake Magic sheets. Place dough ball between the sheets and roll, readjusting plastic if dough begins to press out as you roll. (Dampen the counter slightly to keep sheets from slipping around on the counter as you roll them.)

4. Spread dried fruit mixture evenly over the surface.

5. Roll out the other ball of dough and place over the top and transfer to a cookie sheet. Place plastic sheet on top and roll firmly to merge layers together.

6. Score (press knife, don't drag). Bake at 350°F for 25 minutes or until golden brown on edges and bottom.

❧ Makes 24 to 32 cookies.

Coconut Macaroons

2 cups unsweetened, flaked coconut

1 cup whole wheat pastry flour or brown rice flour

2 tablespoons cornstarch

1 teaspoon salt

1½ cups raw carrot pieces or diced apple

2 tablespoons sugar (optional)

⅓ cup honey, warmed slightly to make it pour

1 teaspoon vanilla

1. Place 1 cup coconut in a food processor with whole wheat or rice flour and salt. Blend with the steel blade for 1 minute.

2. Add diced apple or carrots and raw sugar, and blend about 20 seconds to blend in the apple.

3. Add the honey and vanilla and blend again about 20 seconds or until all is mixed.

4. Scoop out dough with a small ice-cream scoop, or drop into mounds on cookie sheet. Flatten, if desired. Bake at 350°F for about 15 minutes. They will be soft, but lightly brown on the bottom. Cool on the cookie sheet. Makes about 20 cookies.

Chewy Oatmeal Cookies

Keeping cookies in the cookie jar makes a happy family happier. I have found that keeping several kinds of cookies on hand in the freezer in Ziploc bags is a great idea—just the thing to take on trips and put in sack lunches.

¾ cup brown sugar

1 cup coconut milk

¾ teaspoon salt

1 cup whole wheat flour

2 teaspoons Ener-G Baking Soda* or 1 teaspoon regular baking powder

1½ cup quick oats

¾ cup raisins

½ cup sliced almonds or chopped walnuts (optional)

1 cup diced fruit such as peaches, apples, pears, crushed pineapple, mangos, or persimmons

1. Combine brown sugar and coconut milk in a mixing bowl, stirring until creamy. Add flour, salt, and baking powder and stir just until mixed. Add remaining ingredients, folding in the fresh fruit last.

2. Scoop onto a cookie sheet with a spoon or small ice-cream scoop. The mix should be soft, but firm enough to stay in small mounds. Flatten slightly with a fork or rubber spatula (dip in water to avoid sticking).

3. Bake for about 15 minutes at 350°F, or until lightly browned on top and bottom.

Makes about 24 cookies.

*If using Ener-G Baking Soda, be sure you have baking soda, not baking powder. (See p. 102—there is an important difference where cookies are concerned!)

ALMOND JEWELS

1 cup whole wheat pastry flour
or 1¼ cups quick oats

2 tablespoons cornstarch

1 teaspoon salt

⅔ cup brown sugar

1 tablespoon **Ener-G Baking Soda**
or 1 teaspoon regular baking powder
or ½ teaspoon baking soda

2 cups raw almonds

½ cup applesauce

¼ cup water

2 teaspoons vanilla

⅓ cup purchased sugarless fruit jam

1. Place flour, cornstarch, salt, brown sugar, baking soda, and 1 cup of the almonds in a food processor and blend for 1 minute, or until nuts are as fine as the flour. Add remaining cup of almonds and blend for about 10 seconds. (Second cup of almonds should be ground to a coarse meal about the texture of whole wheat berries.)

2. Remove to a mixing bowl and stir in the remaining ingredients except for the fruit jam.

3. Spoon onto a cookie sheet (or use a small ice-cream scoop). Make a thumb indentation in the center of each cookie and fill each depression with fruit jam.

4. Bake at 350°F for about 15 minutes. Remove when the bottoms are just beginning to brown. Cool on a rack.

Makes about 20 cookies.

CRUNCHY CLUSTERS

This recipe was our best seller at Five Loaves Deli. People loved the whole grain nutrition mixed with the delicate sweet flavor of rice syrup. It was something quick and easy to eat on the run. Children loved them, and we think you will too! See picture on page 76.

1 cup brown rice syrup or corn syrup

¼ cup honey

1 teaspoon vanilla

1 tablespoon molasses

½ teaspoon butter-flavored salt (or salt)

8 cups puffed whole-grain cereal *(rice, corn, millet, or wheat—a mixture is good; we have even tried Kix cereal mixed in)*

½ cup each: sesame seeds, slivered almonds, sunflower seeds, dry-roasted peanuts *(may use just peanuts or sesame seeds or other nuts)*

3 tablespoons peanut butter

1. Place brown rice syrup, honey, vanilla, molasses, and salt in a saucepan and bring to boil. Reduce heat and simmer 10 minutes; then stir in peanut butter.

2. Combine puffed cereal and nuts in a large mixing bowl. Add hot syrup, mix together.

3. Wet hands and press entire mix firmly into an oiled 12" x 17" sheet pan. Bake at 350°F until golden brown (about 10 minutes—be careful, it burns easily). Remove from oven and let cool about 10 minutes. Then scribe with a knife into squares while still warm. Cool and break.

Hint: Removing the baked clusters from the cookie sheet can be a challenge unless the pan has been well greased. I always use a sheet of Bake Magic on my pan, and there is no sticking and no grease!

POPCORN OR POPCORN BALLS

1. Make 1 gallon of unseasoned popcorn, and add some peanuts if desired.

2. Simmer rice syrup mixture on the stove for 10 minutes or to the "soft ball" stage. (With a spoon, dribble a few drops of boiling mix into cold water. A ball should form, soft to the touch.)

3. Quickly pour the hot liquid over the popcorn and mix lightly with a large spoon. Coat hands with oil; scoop up and press coated popcorn together lightly into round balls.

Hint: Make low-fat popcorn with a hot-air popper. (Season by drizzling with olive oil and sprinkling with Flavacol or salt.)

LEMON BALLS

Children will love helping you make this simple recipe—and they'll love eating the lemon balls too!

1 cup dried pineapple pieces (low sugar)

1 cup golden raisins

¾ cup raw cashew nuts

⅛ teaspoon lemon extract

¼ teaspoon salt

¼ cup fine coconut

1. Put all ingredients except coconut in food processor. Whiz for about 1 minute. At first the ingredients will remain crumbly and separate; then they will begin to stick together in a ball. Continue whizzing about 15 more seconds to chop and blend together.

2. Place fine coconut in a bowl. Scoop out fruit mixture a tablespoon at a time and shape into a ball with your hands, then roll in coconut and place balls in a flat storage container. Chill before serving.

Tip: A small (4-ounce) ice-cream scoop works great for this! Scoop out and release into the coconut. Shape balls as you roll them in the coconut.

Variation: *Try other dried fruits or nuts, such as dried apricots, cranberries, cherries, dates, almonds, or walnuts.*

Makes about 16 1-inch balls.

TAPIOCA PUDDING

We had to include this favorite recipe from Best Gourmet Recipes. *This was one dessert we didn't dare run out of at Five Loaves. If we did, there would always be some disappointed customers. It is a light and refreshing dessert that fits just about any occasion. My thanks to Rilla Klingbeil for introducing this recipe to us.*

1 cup raw almonds

1¼ cups water

¼ cup tapioca

1 teaspoon vanilla

1 teaspoon coconut extract

½ teaspoon salt

⅓ cup honey or ½ cup sugar

3 cups water

1. Blend almonds and water for about 1 minute. Add 3 cups water and blend briefly.

2. Place a cloth-lined sieve over a kettle and pour the blended almonds and water through the cloth. Close up cloth securely around the almond pulp and squeeze out as much of the milk as you can. Discard pulp.

Hint: Instead of sieve, use nut milk bag if available (see Glossary).

3. Add remaining ingredients to almond milk in kettle and stir occasionally while bringing to a boil. When it is barely beginning to boil (steam is rising and first little bubble rises), remove from heat, place in shallow container, and

cool quickly in the refrigerator. Over-boiling will result in a less-desirable thick and gummy consistency.

Hint: Altitude and humidity will affect the needed boiling time. While boiling too much gives a poor result, higher altitude or humidity will require more boiling, even as long as 1 full minute. It may take some experimenting to get it just right for your area. Too little boiling results in a pudding that is too runny.

4. An attractive serving idea is to layer the pudding in tall glass dessert dishes with small spoonfuls of Fresh Raspberry Jam (p. 59), and/or Blueberry Fruit Sauce (p. 17).

Makes 4½ cups.

(May use cashew nuts instead of almonds; no need to strain, but almonds give this a nicer taste.)

PISTACHIO PUDDING BARS

Here's another dessert from Kimberley's kitchen. She wanted to make a custardlike texture (but without eggs) that would keep its shape when cut and resemble a delicious dessert she had made from a mix.

- 2 cups almond or coconut milk
- 3 tablespoons honey or ¼ cup sugar
- ¼ teaspoon salt
- 1 teaspoon vanilla
- 1 teaspoon almond extract
- 1½ tablespoons cornstarch
- 1½ tablespoons regular Clear Jel or 2 teaspoons potato starch (cornstarch makes it sliceable; Clear Jel or potato starch for custard consistency)
- 1 or 2 drops green food coloring
- ½ cup chopped pistachio nuts (optional)
- Crumble Nut Crust in 9-inch square baking dish (p. 83)

1. Make ½ recipe almond milk according to directions in Tapioca Pudding (p. 96), steps 1 and 2.

Tip: Best with almond, but coconut milk can be substituted. Coconut milk will vary in richness depending on the source or brand—dilute with water to obtain the richness you desire.

2. Place all ingredients in blender and blend about 30 seconds. Pour into a saucepan and bring to a boil, stirring constantly as it thickens. Remove from heat and add food coloring if used.

3. Pour into the prebaked crust. Chill several hours before serving. Top with Whipped Topping (p. 99), if desired, and garnish with nuts.

❧Makes 9 servings.

VANILLA CUSTARD

Use Pistachio Pudding Bars recipe, omitting almond extract and green food color. Chill and serve with Fresh Raspberry Jam (p. 59) or Carob Sauce (p. 99) and chopped nuts. Or top with fresh or frozen berries. Makes an excellent filling for Fruit Pizza (p. 86).

Quick Pudding Option: Blend 10-ounce box soft MoriNu Tofu with ½ cup cashews, 1 teaspoon vanilla, ½ cup sugar, and ¼ teaspoon salt

CAROB PUDDING OR CUSTARD

Use Pistachio Pudding Bars recipe, omitting green food coloring and pistachio nuts. Blend in 2 tablespoons carob powder, ½ teaspoon Roma or other coffee substitute.

PEACHY TRIFLE DESSERT CUP

1 recipe Whipped Topping (p. 99)

1 recipe Create-a-Cake (p. 79) (use
    applesauce and no nuts or raisins)

1 recipe Lemon Cream Pie filling
    (p. 87) or Vanilla Custard (p. 97)

2 cups fresh raspberries or Fresh
    Raspberry Jam (p. 59)

2 fresh peaches or other fruit in season

1-2 cups fresh blueberries (optional)

**1. Day ahead: Make Whipped Topping
and chill. Make cake; store in plastic bag.**

**2. 4-8 hours ahead: Cut cake in 1-inch
cubes, and scatter half of the cubes
over the bottom of a glass casserole or
a deep, straight-sided glass trifle
bowl, or individual dessert glasses.
Make Lemon Cream Pie filling, and
pour over the cake in the dish. Scatter
remaining cake and press lightly into
the filling. Cover and chill overnight
or for at least 1 hour.**

**3. An hour before serving, slice peaches
and arrange along the sides of the bowl
so they show. Layer with Whipped Topping, fresh raspberries, or Raspberry**

Jam. Top with blueberries and fresh
raspberries or peach slices. Chill and
serve.

CAROB DESSERT TRIFLE

Place two or three shortcake cubes in
a dessert dish, and top with Vanilla
Custard (p. 97), Carob Sauce (p. 99),
and fresh or frozen raspberries. Or top
shortcake cubes with Carob Pudding
(p. 97), Whipped Topping (p. 99), and
frozen raspberries or Fresh Raspberry
Jam (p. 59).

WHIPPED TOPPING

This is something better than Cool Whip. Delicious on pie, pudding, or spread on cake like icing. This creamy topping can also be used in a pastry tube or plastic squeeze bottle for decorating. See picture on the left.

- 1 cup water
- 2 tablespoons agar flakes (2 teaspoons powder)
- ½ cup raw cashew nuts
- ⅓ cup honey or ½ cup sugar
- ½ teaspoon salt
- 1 teaspoon vanilla
- ½ teaspoon coconut extract
- ¼ teaspoon xanthan gum (optional, but especially nice in icing)
- 1 can coconut milk (or 2 cups soy milk)

1. **Stir together the agar and water, and bring to a boil, stirring constantly. Reduce heat and simmer for 1-2 minutes.**

2. **Place remaining ingredients in blender along with hot agar mixture. Blend on high until smooth, adding water as needed to make 3½ to 4 cups total mixture (3½ cups total mixture for icing; 4 cups for whipped topping). Pour into a quart container and chill in refrigerator several hours or overnight. For quicker chilling, use a large, shallow container.**

Hint: Since this recipe needs blending twice, leave the blended mixture (step 2) in the blender in the refrigerator overnight. Then simply reblend as in step 3, saving the work of washing the blender and containers twice!

3. **Before using, place chilled mixture (which will be quite firm—almost sliceable) in blender or food processor, and blend until creamy. (If you have a lightweight blender, you should blend just half of the mix at a time.) It should be the consistency of Cool Whip, and spreads on a cake very nicely. Try not to add more liquid. The mixture will eventually go through the blades and become creamy if you carefully push it toward the blades with a rubber spatula.**

The agar is a key ingredient in this recipe. The mixture has to be reblended only once. Then it can be frozen and used without reblending, but remains a nice creamy texture. So make a double recipe and freeze in small containers to use as needed for icing or dessert topping.

☙*Makes 6 cups*

FIVE LOAVES RICE CREAM

During our 10 years of operation we always served this recipe in our soft-serve machine. It can be made in a blender, but is easiest to make in the kind of ice-cream maker that has a container you keep in the freezer. (Cuisinart makes a good one.) When ready to use, simply mount the freezer container on the motor, turn on, and pour in the mix. In 20 minutes you have soft ice cream ready to serve. Picture is on page 78.

- ¾ cup cashew nuts
- ½ cup cooked brown rice*
- ½ cup pitted dates
- ½ cup fruit juice sweetener or honey
- ½ teaspoon salt
- 1 teaspoon vanilla
- ½ teaspoon guar gum or xanthan gum (optional)
- 2 cups water
- ice cubes (optional, about 1 tray)

*If desired, you may omit the rice and increase nuts to 1 cup cashew nuts.

1. **Blend all the ingredients (except ice cubes) in a blender until very smooth (may take up to 2 minutes). There should be no grittiness when a drop of mixture is felt between your thumb and finger.**

2. **Add ice cubes and blend smooth (speeds chilling time). Add more water as needed to make 5 cups total mix.**

3. **Pour into ice-cream maker and freeze according to its directions. (Or pour into a shallow pan and freeze. When ready to use, thaw slightly until just soft enough to cut into squares. Place in a blender with enough soy milk or water to blend into the consistency of soft ice cream.)**

4. **Spoon into containers as soon as the mix is done (if the ice cream is left in an ice-cream maker, some will freeze to the container and become hard). Store in freezer until ready to use.**

Hint: This ice-cream recipe will harden more in the freezer than store-bought high-fat brands. To serve, thaw slightly in the microwave.

☙*Makes 6 cups.*

COCONUT ICE CREAM

This recipe makes a very creamy textured ice cream that is guaranteed to please anyone!

- 1 can coconut milk (or use 3 cups soy milk instead and omit the 1 cup water)

- 1 cup water
- ½ cup raw cashew nuts
- ½ cup pitted dates
- ½ cup honey (⅔ cup sugar may be used in place of the dates and honey)
- 2 teaspoons vanilla
- ½ teaspoon salt
- ½ teaspoon guar or xanthan gum (optional)
- 1 tray ice cubes
- water as needed to make 5 cups total mixture

Follow directions for Five Loaves Rice Cream.

☙*Makes 6 cups.*

CAROB SAUCE

- ½ cup date pieces
- ½ cup honey
- ½ cup hot water
- ¼ cup cashew nuts
- 2 tablespoons carob powder
- 1 teaspoon vanilla
- ½ teaspoon Roma coffee substitute
- ½ teaspoon salt

Blend together until smooth. Serve over ice cream or Vanilla Custard (p. 97).

☙*Makes 2 cups.*

Preparing meals from whole plant foods is not just a theory with us—it has been our lifestyle for 35 years. If it is new to you, it probably seems like you will have to spend your life in the kitchen. But with experience you will discover how easy it really is. In this section we will share some of the secrets we have learned to make the job more efficient.

ORGANIZE YOUR PANTRY

Think of a place you can put often-used ingredients where they will be handy. I once visited in the home of a friend who cooks this way and likes to be organized. She had a small kitchen drawer that she would pull open, and there were rows of 4-ounce pimento jars on their sides, labeled and filled with such items as: Chicken-Like Seasoning, Beef-Like Seasoning, corn starch, agar, xanthan gum, yeast flakes, Clear Jel, butter-flavored salt, Ener-G Baking Powder, potato flour, ranch dressing mix, bean seasoning, tofu seasoning, etc. She had larger containers of those things in another place from which she would refill the small containers in her drawer when they got low. I was impressed! But saving enough pimento jars takes time, and not long after that I saw a sale on little plastic jars with snap lids that filled the bill perfectly for me. Now I have a handy drawer too, and it has ended the trips to this or that cupboard, looking behind things, or scrambling through bags of things to find what I need.

Elsewhere, you need a place for other larger amounts of such staples as beans, rice, dates, etc. I keep mine in gallon jars on the bottom shelf of my pantry. We live in a dry climate where food weevils are not very common. I have an extra refrigerator and freezer in the garage where I keep plastic storage bags of nuts and flour.

CONTAINER CATASTROPHE

The years of restaurant work left its stamp on the three of us. Kathy and Kimberley learned, as I did, how important it is to have plenty of storage containers. At Five Loaves we had the usual stacks of cup, pint, and quart plastic containers with lids that you get at restaurant supply stores. They stack in neat columns and rows, one lid fits all, and they are inexpensive. My kitchen at home was small, and I got rid of my hodgepodge of containers I had been hoarding for years in my cramped cupboard, and replaced them with the neat stacks of plastic restaurant containers. This is one of the best things I have done to

make my kitchen work go smoothly. The only other storage containers I have are one dozen flat, square containers with lids, and several large Rubbermaid containers.

FREEZE IT

Having a large freezer is really a time saver. Recipes often make more than can be eaten at a meal. The extra can be frozen and pulled out at times when you don't have time to cook.

I usually have these in my freezer:

Simple Cheese Sauce (p. 26) for pizza, pizza crusts

Sliceable Cashew Cheese (p. 73) (for grating)

Whipped Topping (p. 99)

containers of leftover homemade ice cream

Simple Gravy (p. 26)

half-cup portions of **Cashew Cream** (p. 107), coconut milk

Oat Burgers (p. 35), **Tofu-Walnut Balls** (p. 41), etc.

servings for one or two of chili or soup

one-cup bags of cooked rice

pizza crusts

cookies

servings for one or two of carrot cake or pie

CUTTING AND SLICING MADE EASY

PARING KNIVES: Make sure to supply your kitchen with good knives. Look for Victorinox serrated paring knives, the kind with a black or red vinyl handle. You can get them at many restaurant supply stores, such as Smart and Final, for very few dollars. (Buy several. Put them on the breakfast table so that everyone will cut and eat plenty of fresh fruit.)

CUTTING BOARDS? A cutting mat is so easy to clean, store, and pour into the kettle or mixing bowl whatever you have chopped. They fit anywhere, and are great for traveling.

ONIONS: Don't slice just one or two green onions at a time; slice a bunch or two, and keep them in a container for a week of use. Same with yellow onions, but keep them in a mason jar with lid so the smell doesn't permeate the rest of the fridge. I buy 1½-pound containers of dehydrated onions at a restaurant supply store. Believe it or not, they are less expensive than fresh onions and so easy to use.

DICED RED PEPPERS: In our restaurant we bought diced red peppers in large cans and kept them in the fridge or freezer to use in cheese sauce or in soups or casseroles. I find it very helpful even in my kitchen for two. You can buy them in smaller, 28-ounce cans, divide them in freezer containers, and keep a cup or two of them in the fridge. You would be surprised how often they are nice to use, even to dress up a simple frozen corn side dish. And they are less expensive and easier than chopping bell peppers.

Handy Mixes You Can Make

Another way to streamline your busy morning is to make mixes for pancakes, muffins, and waffles. It might not seem necessary at first glance, but I am reminded every time I pull out my waffle mix how much easier and quicker it is to make waffles when I have this handy mix all ready to use. It's much quicker to measure out of one bag instead of pulling five or six ingredients out of my pantry and freezer.

Waffle Mix

8 cups quick oatmeal

2 cups cornmeal or millet (or 1 of each)

2 cups cashew pieces

2 cups flaxseed

1 cup cornstarch

4 teaspoons salt

Mix together thoroughly in a large mixing bowl and pour into a plastic storage bag. Store in freezer or refrigerator. After several uses, you should know how much to make for your family, or just for 1-2 people.

Waffle Mix Recipe For Two

2 cups water

1 tablespoon apple or orange juice concentrate or 2 teaspoons honey or 1 pitted date

1¾ cups waffle mix

Place all in blender and blend until smooth—at least 1 minute. Pour into hot waffle iron and bake until done. Makes two large waffles.

Whole Wheat Pancake and Muffin Mix

2 cups Brazil nuts or walnuts

12 cups whole wheat flour

⅔ cup cornstarch

1 cup **Ener-G Baking Powder** (or ½ cup regular)

1 cup **Sucanat** or ¾ cup sugar (or use honey with water when ready to mix and bake)

2 tablespoons salt

1. Place 1 cup nuts and 1 cup flour in food processor and whiz for 1 minute until nuts are as fine as the flour. Repeat with the second cup of nuts. (If you have a large food processor, you can process 2 cups nuts with 2 cups flour.)

2. Pour blended nut-and-flour mixture into a large bowl and add the remaining ingredients.

3. Mix together and store in a plastic storage bag in the freezer.

Multigrain Pancake and Muffin Mix

You can make a delicious multigrain mix. Follow **Pancake Mix** recipe above, replacing 12 cups whole wheat flour with the following:

2 cups quick oats

4 cups whole wheat flour

2 cups brown rice flour

2 cups barley flour

1 cup rye flour

Pancakes From Mix

1. Preheat a nonstick skillet to medium temperature.

2. Place 1 cup pancake mix in a mixing bowl and add 1 cup water.

3. Ladle onto hot griddle in ¼-cup portions. Bake until golden brown on each side.

Muffins From Mix

2¼ cups **Pancake** or **Muffin Mix**

1¼ cups water

replace ½ cup water with ½ cup mashed banana, applesauce, or pumpkin if desired

¼ cup honey

½ cup raisins or blueberries (optional)

½ cup nuts (optional)

Mix and spoon into muffin tin. Bake at 350°F about 25 minutes. Makes 9-12 muffins.

Piecrust Mix

3 cups flour (barley, whole wheat pastry, or unbleached white)

3 cups quick oats

4 cups Brazil nuts or walnuts

4½ teaspoons salt

Place flour, nuts, and salt in a food processor and blend about 1 minute, until nuts have been ground as fine as the flour. Store in plastic bag in freezer.

Hint: For a single piecrust, use 1 cup mix and follow directions on page 83 for Simple and Flaky Piecrust.

Does your family enjoy Tofu Scramble With Vegetables (p. 24) for breakfast? The job will seem less daunting if you have the seasoning all ready to go. Here's a great mix to help with that.

Tofu Seasoning

½ cup **Chicken-Like Seasoning**

1¼ cups food yeast flakes

¼ cup garlic powder

¾ cup onion powder

¾ teaspoon turmeric

Mix together and store in an airtight container. Use 3 tablespoons seasoning and 1 tablespoon Bragg Liquid Aminos with 16 ounces firm tofu, crumbled.

It took me quite a while to learn how to make good-tasting meals using whole foods. So don't be too hard on yourself if you don't suceed right away. Take one step at a time. Learn to make one recipe at a time. Success in the little steps will one day find you preparing wholesome meals as effortlessly as driving a car.

Some of the recipes in this cookbook might contain an ingredient or two that you have never heard of, probably because they aren't found in regular supermarkets. You'll have to go off the beaten path a little to find certain "secret" ingredients that help improve your family's health.

Here is a list of not-so-common ingredients, with some help on how to find them. If you have the ingredients at your fingertips you are not so likely to fall back on old habits. So make a list and venture out to your local natural food store, where many of these ingredients can be found. To save time, show your list to a clerk who can help you find things. You need to do all you can to eliminate frustration and turn this experience into an enjoyable adventure.

Today, trucking, shipping, and Internet shopping have made rare items accessible to almost everyone. You will find sources at the end of this section for online or phone ordering if you can't find these products locally.

Agar

This comes from the algae "agar-agar." It is rich in calcium, iron, phosphorus, and vitamins. Used mainly as a thickener, agar is an excellent vegan substitute for gelatin, which is an animal product. Far superior to traditional gelatin, which offers few health benefits, it can be used in much the same way gelatin is used—but needs to boil longer for good results. It comes in several forms—flakes, powder, sticks, or bundles of strands. Available in most Asian food stores or natural food stores. See page 106 for equivalents.

Bake Magic

It's a reusable nonstick liner for baking sheets and pans, replacing parchment paper. Made of Teflon-coated fiberglass, it can be wiped clean and is dishwasher-safe. Can be cut to fit muffin cups (unlike silicone baking sheets, which cannot be cut). Safe to 500°F. As seen in New York *Times*, Los Angeles *Times*, *Bon Appetit,* and others. The sheet measures 18" x 14½".

> www.shopwithease.com
> 800-336-1968

Baking Powder, Ener-G

Made simply of calcium carbonate and citric acid. Use it in proportions about two times that of regular baking powder and bake soon after mixing, as the rising begins as soon as it is mixed. Carried in some natural food stores, but you will probably have to order it by mail. Ener-G Foods, P.O. Box 24723, Seattle, WA 98124.

> www.ener-g.com
> 206-767-6660

Baking Soda, Ener-G

The only ingredient is calcium carbonate (no citric acid), so gives less rise to baked goods. I use it sometimes in cookies, because cookie dough is stiff and the citric acid in Ener-G Baking Powder doesn't "gas out," leaving a detectable sour taste.

Baking Powder, Rumford

A baking powder that is made without aluminum, but does contain baking soda.

Bragg Liquid Aminos

Made from soybeans, is similar to soy sauce, but not as strong and not fermented. It is sold in health food stores. For more information, write: Live Food Products, Box 7, Santa Barbara, CA 93102.

Brown Rice Syrup

This cultured product is made from brown rice, water, and a small amount of natural cereal enzyme. The light and delicate syrup is about half as sweet as sugar.

Bulgur Wheat

Precooked and dried cracked wheat. Gives a meaty texture to some of our entrées.

Butter Salt (McCormick's or Flavacol)

Most of them have objectionable ingredients, but I have used McCormick's to flavor my butter. Now I use a popcorn salt called Flavacol. It contains only salt, artificial butter flavor, and color. It comes in a quart-sized paper milk carton and is found in the popcorn section of restaurant supply stores. A big carton of it is less expensive than a little bottle of McCormick's. It is nice to use in other dishes where a butter flavor is needed. I especially like it in **Tofu Scramble With Vegetables** (p. 24), and along with food yeast flakes and onion powder it makes a perfect substitute for chicken seasoning. See page 107 for recipe. Flavacol Popcorn Salt is manufactured by Gold Medal, Cincinnati, Ohio.

> www.gmpopcorn.com
> 800-543-0862
> You can order it online at Home Theater Express:
> www.ht-express.com

California Chili

Made from a mild, dried chili pepper. Found in Mexican aisles of supermarkets.

Carob Powder

Made from the locust pod, carob powder has a fat content of 2 percent as compared to chocolate's 52 percent. It is high in calcium, phosphorus, potassium, iron, magnesium, and other minerals and vitamins. Tastes enough like chocolate to be used as a substitute. It is not bitter and therefore requires less sugar than chocolate to make it sweet. All brands of cocoa, from which chocolate is made, contain more tannin per cup than tea, which has approximately 2 grains per cup. Caffeine and theobromine (an alkaloid cousin to caffeine) may cause headaches, central nervous system irritation, general or localized itching, depression, and anxiety. Caffeine content per cup of cocoa beverage is low (27 cups of chocolate drink equal a cup of brewed coffee). Carob contains no tannin, caffeine, or theobromine. May be purchased from most natural food stores.

Chicken-Like or Beef-Like Seasoning

Our favorites have been McKay's or Bill's Best. Both make a chicken or beef flavor that is without animal fat. McKay's can be purchased without MSG. A vegan version that contains no hydrogenated oil is also available. If you can't find them in a health food store, both can be ordered by mail from any of the online sources found on page 105. Or order Bill's Best directly from Nutri-Line Foods, Box 33, Paradise, CA 95967. Another good one is made by Butler Foods (see page 104 under Soy Curls). Or try our **Homemade Chicken-Like Seasoning** on page 107.

> 503-876-0823
> www.nutrilinefoods.com

Clear Jel, Instant

Hybrid waxy corn, this starch has a modified molecular structure and is precooked to thicken upon contact with cold liquid. It should be blended rather than stirred into your preparation—it's an excellent way to thicken cold fruit sauces (doesn't work with heat). Some natural food stores carry it, but it's one of those items that is usually found only at a bakery supply or wholesale grocers' outlet in 25-pound bags. Can be purchased from Weimar Institute's Weimart.

> 877-934-6278
> www.weimar.org

Clear Jel, Regular

Very similar to the instant version though not precooked (looks just like cornstarch), this has to be heated to become thick. It is superior to cornstarch for cooked fruit sauces because it retains its silky, smooth texture, hot or cold. Cornstarch-thickened sauces become jellylike when cooled, or, if then stirred, have a rough texture. Bakers use a similar product called modified food starch to achieve that beautiful satin look for jelly-roll fillings or cheesecake toppings. Can be purchased through Weimar Institute's Weimart.

> 877-934-6278
> www.weimar.org

Coconut Milk

I usually buy this in Asian stores for less than half the price it costs in supermarkets. In a supermarket you'll find it in the Asian section. Cheap brands include starch as an ingredient, which means it has been diluted and won't work as well in cakes and cookies. I have also found that brands vary in richness. Coconut milk is made by blending coconut meat with water and pressing out the milk through a sieve; there seems to be no consistency between brands for the amount of water used. You can tell the milk is rich if it is thick like cream instead of thin like milk. I use the richer brand for replacing shortening in baked goods, while less-rich brands may be used to replace milk in cream sauces or soups. Research has shown that coconut meat is not atherogenic. (Pure coconut oil is partly because of the loss of phytochemicals in the refining process when producing oil.) All recipes in this book use a 13.5-ounce can (1¾ cups).

Coriander

The green herb is cilantro, but the seed of the plant is called coriander. Usually ground into a powder and used in Indian curries. Nice to use in place of cinnamon—a spice we have all learned to love, but an irritating substance it would be prudent to avoid.

Dates

Date pieces coated with oat flour are very handy for cooking and baking. Dates of any shape can be used, but if they're dry and hard you should rinse them with water and leave in an airtight container several hours. For quick use, boil them. They can be found in most natural food stores or purchased in bulk from natural food co-ops.

Dough Conditioner

I have not used it until recently—mainly because I was uncertain about the ingredients. But we recently found one that had acceptable ingredients and tried it with wonderful results. Use it in **Sweet Rolls** (p. 65) and **Cobbler Crust** (p. 88) to make them lighter. An improved dough conditioner is manufactured by Caravan, a kosher company in New Jersey. The ingredients are as follows: wheat flour, datem (an emulsifier derived from soy to give strength to the dough), l-cysteine, enzyme, ascorbic acid, and azodicarbonamide (ADA).

Flavacol Popcorn Salt

See Butter Salt

Flaxseed

Shiny reddish-brown seed, slightly larger than sesame seeds. Soft enough to grind easily into a meal in a seed mill or blender. Makes a good replacement for eggs when blended into recipes and is a great antioxidant.

Fructose

This natural sugar, which is 50 percent sweeter than table sugar (sucrose), is used in a few of the dessert recipes where extra sweetening is needed without extra liquid. Refined from fruit but nutritionally little better.

Fruit Juice Sweetener

This is now used by many bakeries and food manufacturers to replace sugar, and can be found in most natural food stores. It is usually made from peach, pear, and pineapple concentrates combined. Its sweetening effect is superior to apple juice concentrate in most recipes because it is has a milder, less acidic taste.

Gluten Flour

It is derived from whole wheat and is the glutenous part of the grain that causes bread to be light and elastic. High in protein and helpful as a binder or for adding to bread flour that has a low gluten content.

Green Ripe Olives

A rare find in conventional supermarkets, I get them from www.vegefoods.com.

Green Soybeans (Edamame)

May be purchased either in or out of the pod. They cook in 5 minutes and make a delightful side dish. People enjoy them in the pod because of the novel way of eating—you squeeze the pod, and out pop the beans!

Masa Harina Flour

Found in the Mexican foods section of many supermarkets. High in nutrition because mostly unrefined. Used for making tortillas and tamales.

Nut Milk Bag

A small mesh bag that makes straining nut milk more efficient. Obtain from www.rawgourmet.com.

Meat Analogs (Meat Replacements)

Usually made from wheat gluten or soy and can be used to replace meat in recipes. Many canned products made by Worthington (Cutlets, Skallops, Vegetarian Burger, Veja-Links, Nuteena) have been available in natural food aisles of supermarkets for many years. Newer products now available in frozen food sections. Lunchmeat slices can be purchased for use in sandwiches. They are tasty and convenient, but label reading is a good idea. Many are high in refined fat and contain soy protein isolate—not a heart-friendly food. See page 37 for recipes for simple homemade replacements to keep in your freezer.

Onion Powder

There are two kinds—granulated onion and fine onion powder. I used to like granulated onion because it mixed into hot liquid without lumping, but later learned that the fine onion powder has a much superior flavor.

Pasta, Whole Grain

Have you tried whole wheat pasta and found it was either too chewy or too mushy? Now there are several brands that are really good. If you are favored with a Trader Joe's near you, their store brand of whole wheat spaghetti is excellent. I recently discovered a brand of brown rice pasta that is very good—Tinkyada PastaJOY. Its claim on the package caught my eye—good, consistent texture, not mushy, al dente. "The good texture of Tinkyada can withstand quite a bit of overcooking." True to its claim, this pasta had a wonderful texture that didn't fall apart like others I have tried in the past! Comes in a variety of shapes and can be found in health food sections of supermarkets or a health food store such as Wild Oats.
   888-323-2388
   www.ricepasta.com

Potato Flour

This is precooked dried potatoes ground into flour. It is great for thickening anything without cooking, but is best to add it in the blender for a smooth product. Usually found in natural food stores, but check the ingredients to be sure it is potato flour and not potato starch (which is like cornstarch and has to be cooked to thicken).

Roma (Coffee Substitute)

Found in some natural food stores, or can be ordered from www.vegefoods.com. A good-tasting coffee substitute that most people who are getting off coffee seem to like. Used in some recipes for a mocha flavor.

Sesame Tahini

Raw or roasted sesame seeds ground into butter. Used in some dressings and spreads.

Soy Curls

A delicious product made from the whole soybean—no additives or preservatives. May be reconstituted and flavored to taste like chicken or beef. Order from Butler Foods, P.O. Box 40, Grand Ronde, OR 97347.
   503-879-5005
   www.butlerfoods.com

Soy Milk Powder

Better Than Milk makes one called Soy Carb Care that does not have added refined fat and is especially formulated for diabetics. Find in health food stores or order at 800-238-3947.

Soy Supreme

Powdered, precooked soybeans (no strong flavor). Can be ordered from Country Life Natural Foods or Weimar Natural Foods (see p. 105). There are two varieties: regular and reduced fiber.

Sucanat

Short for "sugar cane natural," Sucanat is made by processing the juice from sugar cane and then dehydrating it.

Tofu

Made from soybean curd. Can be found in the produce section of most supermarkets. I use extra firm for slicing; firm for scrambled tofu or blending. I keep the small, pasteurized boxes of tofu (MoriNu) on hand too, and like them blended with cashew nuts for a rich, smooth dressing or mayonnaise. I always buy soft MoriNu because the firm tofu has soy protein isolate added—not a very heart-friendly food!

Vege-Sal

A very nice vegetable seasoning that is handy to use when you're making any savory dish that needs more flavor, but you're not sure what it needs. Found in natural food stores.

Wright's Hickory Seasoning

A liquid flavoring found in a dark-brown bottle. Look for it in the seasoning section of your supermarket. Usually grouped with A-1 Sauce, etc.

Xanthan Gum and Guar Gum

Xanthan gum and guar gum are generally found in most health food stores and are used as substitutes for fat in many commercial products because they mimic its texture.

Yeast Flakes, Nutritional

Good nutritional yeast flakes are yellow and have a gentle, cheeselike flavor. Good for gravies and sauces. Also good on popcorn. Not to be confused with the brown, powdered brewer's yeast, which is very bitter; nor the active dry yeast used to raise bread.

Where to Buy Natural Foods

Here are some companies that produce and/or distribute high-quality natural foods. If you are unable to find an item at your local store, call or write for catalogs. Also check online for a list of products available by mail. You can also use our Web site for a source or links to others: www.bestgourmetrecipes.org.

Weimar Institute is a health-conditioning center that specializes in reversing heart disease and diabetes. They have an on-campus store, The Weimart, that carries almost every hard-to-find item on your shopping list, including Clear Jel (Instant and Regular).

Weimar Natural Foods
P.O. Box 486
Weimar, California 95736
　877-934-6278
　www.weimar.org (Weimart)

(a good source for East Coast)
Country Life Natural Foods
P.O. Box 489
Pullman, Michigan 40450
　800-456-7694
　www.clnf.org

(a good source for bulk nuts in the West)
Azure Standard Quality Bulk and Natural Foods
79709 Dufur Valley Road
Dufur, Oregon 97021
　541-467-2230
　www.azurestandard.com

Ener-G Foods

This firm specializes in products for allergy-restricted diets—especially wheat-free or gluten-intolerant needs. This is the source for Ener-G Baking Powder.

Ener-G Foods, Inc.
P.O. Box 24723
Seattle, Washington 98124
　206-767-6660
　www.ener-g.com

Sweeteners: Sugar/ Honey—Which Should I Buy?

It is estimated that each person in the United States consumes more than 100 pounds a year of sugar—about a pound every 3 days. It's clear that we need to cut back dramatically on our sugar intake. And it can be done if you proceed wisely. Remember this important principle: When you remove something, always replace it with "something better."

We have included a large section of desserts in this book to help you find good, healthful replacements that your family can enjoy—in moderation. We don't recommend complete abstinence, and the reason for that was stated very nicely by Edith Young Cottrell, research nutritionist from Loma Linda University, in her now-classic book, *Oats, Peas, Beans, and Barley Cookbook*.

"Sugar is not a poison as some people say. *As it occurs in nature*, in dilute form and accompanied by the minerals and vitamins necessary for its use by the body, it is a wholesome energy food.

"Moderate amounts of concentrated sugars for flavoring when used with a well-balanced diet containing ample minerals and vitamins will not be harmful to the normal person. But the rich cakes and pastries high in sugar are not wholesome for any person at any time.

"Sugar when eaten alone has the quickest gastric emptying time. Sugar ferments readily when held in the stomach by foods such as fats. . . . This causes a sour stomach and indigestion.

"In addition it is extreme concentration and lack of the essential vitamins and minerals that make sugar a health hazard. This applies also to the less highly refined sugars. Even in the process of concentrating honey, the bees do not pack in enough of the elements really necessary for use by the body.

"Honey is a wholesome food when used in moderation with a diet of unrefined foods high in the necessary minerals and vitamins. Thus it has been used throughout countless ages. Its excessive use with refined foods is not so wholesome" (pp. 129, 130).

You will see that we often use honey instead of sugar. In many places honey is very expensive, and a possible replacement could be brown sugar, though there is only a slight advantage over table sugar. Also, both honey and brown sugar have a stronger taste than white sugar, putting a certain automatic brake on their use. White sugar, in contrast, has a way of sneaking in all over the place, and giving the food such a sweet appeal that you have a hard time resisting seconds and thirds. Desserts that are less sweet will make it easier to eat temperately.

Cashew Nuts

Tofu may be used in place of cashew nuts in creamy recipes. If the recipe calls for ½ cup cashews blended in ½ cup water, use ½ cup firm tofu (4 ounces) blended with ½ cup water, or ¾ cup soft tofu (6 ounces) blended with ¼ cup water.

Almonds may be used cup for cup, but they do not blend as smooth, and the brown skin will give a slightly tan color to the food. But because the flavor is so neutral, we like to use them for certain recipes where a delicate flavor is needed, such as **Tapioca Pudding** (p. 96). In that case we blend them in water, skins included, and strain through a fine cloth (a clean pillow slip works great).

Coconut milk or soy milk can often be used instead of cashew nuts. Replace the water in the recipe with coconut or soy milk and omit the nuts.

Coconut Milk

Coconut milk may be replaced with soy milk for lower calories. Or replace coconut milk with **Cashew Cream** (p. 107) in pastries or baked goods in which the higher fat is needed for tenderness. All recipes in this book use a 13.5-ounce can (1¾ cups).

Tofu

Soaked soybeans (see instructions, p. 107) may be used in place of tofu in recipes that will be cooked or baked, such as **Tofu-Walnut Balls** (p. 41). Blend 1 cup soaked soybeans in 1 cup water and use in place of the tofu.

In dressings or mayonnaise, tofu is used to make a thick, creamy base. This can be replaced with cooked, blended millet or rice—1 cup well-cooked millet or rice, blended with ½ cup water. Add ½ cup nuts or unsweetened coconut (or use some coconut milk in place of some of the water) to give natural fat and flavor.

Baking Powder Equivalents

1 tablespoon **Ener-G Baking Powder**

or 2 teaspoons **Rumford Baking Powder**

or 1½ teaspoons **Calumet** or other double-acting baking powder

Sweetener Equivalents

½ cup honey

or ⅔ cup **Date Sweetener** (p. 107)

or ¾ cup sugar and ½ cup water

or ¾ cup brown sugar and ½ cup water

or ¾ cup crystalized cane juice and ½ cup water

or 1 cup **Sucanat** and ½ cup water

Replace ½ cup sugar or brown sugar with ⅓ cup honey or ½ cup Date Sweetener. Then reduce the water or liquid in the recipe by the amount of honey or Date Sweetener used. It is best to warm the honey briefly (microwave is easy), to make it as runny as water so it mixes into the dry ingredients with the same results as water. If the recipe doesn't call for any other liquid, a dry sweetener should be used.

Seasoning Equivalents

1 tablespoon **Chicken-Like Seasoning**
    or 2 teaspoons food yeast flakes and 1 teaspoon butter-flavored salt
    or 1½ teaspoons salt

1 tablespoon **Bragg's Liquid Aminos**
    or 2 teaspoons soy sauce
    or 1 teaspoon salt

1 tablespoon **Beef-Like Seasoning**
    or 1 package **George Washington Broth**
    or 2 teaspoons soy sauce and 1 tablespoon food yeast flakes
    or 1½ teaspoons salt and 1 tablespoon food yeast flakes

See **Homemade Chicken-Like Seasoning** (p. 107).

Nut Equivalents

1 cup raw cashew nuts
    or 1 cup almonds
    or 1 cup sunflower seeds
    or 1 cup dry-roasted peanuts
    or ⅔ cup Brazil nuts
    or ⅔ cup walnuts
    or ⅔ cup pecans
    or 1½ cups soaked soybeans
    or ¾ cup coconut milk

If making a cream sauce or gravy using cashew nuts (1 cup nuts to 4 cups liquid), cut the amount of added starch in half. Cashews have starch in them, which, when blended, adds to the thickening quality of the sauce.

Equivalent thickening effect from starch or gelatin products

Starch—Add to 1 Cup Liquid

	Cornstarch	Clear Jel	Flour	Potato Starch
Thin	4 tsp.	1 tbsp.	1½ tbsp.	½ tbsp.
Medium	2 tbsp.	1½ tbsp.	2½ tbsp.	1 tbsp.
Thick	2½ tbsp.	2 tbsp.	3 tbsp.	1½ tbsp.

Gelatin—Add to 1 Cup Liquid

	Powdered Agar	Flaked Agar	Agar Sticks	Emes	Knox
Semi-set sliceable pie	½ tsp.	½ tbsp.	⅓	½ tbsp.	½ tbsp.
Stiff Jell-O effect	1 tsp.	1 tbsp.	⅔	1 tbsp.	1 tbsp.
Boiling Time	1 min.	1½ min.	2 min.	bring to boil	bring to boil

REPLACEMENT RECIPES

CASHEW CREAM
    1 cup raw cashew nuts

    1 cup water

Place in blender and blend on high for 2 minutes until smooth.

Double the recipe and keep in small containers in the freezer. This is a good idea because often only a small amount is needed, and it is hard to blend a small amount of cashews into a smooth cream in most blenders. Almonds or other nuts my be used if color is not an issue.

DATE SWEETENER

Blend until smooth: 1 cups dates, 1 cup honey, 1 cup apple juice concentrate. Keep in refrigerator and use like honey in recipes.

HOW TO SOAK SOYBEANS

Wash 1 cup of raw soybeans and cover with 2 cups water and let sit 8 hours. Drain, rinse, and use. Better yet, soak 6 cups in 12 cups water, then freeze in 1-cup amounts in small plastic bags for instant use when needed.

HOMEMADE CHICKEN-LIKE SEASONING
    ¼ cup fine food yeast flakes

    2 tablespoons Flavacol (p. 102)

    2 tablespoons onion powder

    1 teaspoon garlic powder

    2 tablespoons fructose or sugar

Mix together and store in airtight container. Use in place of Chicken-Like Seasoning.

HELPFUL KITCHEN TOOLS

Almost every discipline, art, or trade has its tools. Many whole foods can be eaten just as they are—fresh from the garden, orchard, or market. But to prepare them in ways that are appetizing and appealing, you will find the following tools very helpful.

1. A good blender
Most household blenders will work in making any of these recipes. I have a Vita-Mix, and am so thankful for it. Its strong motor and large capacity not only make the job much easier, but it blends smoother sauces in less time. Most people hesitate at the high price, but when you think of the tools and toys in most of our households (and the prices we are willing to pay for them) it really isn't that much. It just seems like a lot because you can buy an ordinary household blender for so much less. However, for most of my married life all I had was a small blender, and all these recipes will work with a small blender if you blend in smaller amounts, and blend long enough to make it smooth.

2. A food processor
I didn't have one for years, but now that I do, I find it a very valuable tool. Many of the recipes in this book use a food processor to combine nuts and flour for baked goods without using oil. A small inexpensive food processor will work for this by blending smaller amounts at a time. But a larger Cuisinart will make the job quicker and easier.

3. A nonstick skillet or electric grill

4. A nonstick saucepan (1½- to 2-quart)

5. Plenty of plastic containers for leftovers—cup, pint, quart
To save space and confusion, get the ones that have lids that all fit the same containers (see p. 100).

6. Cookie sheets, either nonstick or Bake Magic liners to fit in them (see p. 102).

7. A nonstick waffle iron—buy a new one if your waffles are sticking, and don't use any nonstick spray. New small waffle irons can be purchased for less than $20 at Wal-Mart. A similar and better-quality model made by Cuisinart can be found in department stores for about $30.

HOW-TO MENUS FOR BEGINNERS

If you are wondering where to start, why not try one of our Menus for Beginners? On the following pages are four weekly menus with shopping lists. The idea for this is inspired by the story of Daniel. "But Daniel resolved not to defile himself with the royal food and wine." Daniel asked permission from the reluctant court official for him and his three friends to eat a vegetarian diet for a 10-day trial period. "At the end of the ten days they looked healthier and better nourished than any of the young men who ate the royal food." Read the whole story in Daniel 1:5-20, NIV.

Give yourself a 10-day test—here are menus from which you can choose. Each set of menus is designed to give two people a week of good eating. If you find it too much for your schedule, you can spread it over two weeks. You will need to set aside part of a day—an evening or morning—to prepare several items ahead to be used throughout the week, including one dessert. Unless otherwise indicated, you will make a whole recipe as given in the book, using the leftover in different ways later.

BEANS, RICE, AND MEXICAN

DESSERT AND RECIPES TO MAKE AHEAD

Cuban Black Beans (p. 49)

Peanut Butter 'n' Honey Cookies (p. 90)

Simple Butter (p. 56)

Tofu Sour Cream, double recipe (p. 58)

1. Make 1 recipe Cuban Black Beans in Crock-pot, or put on to soak the night before.

2. Make Peanut Butter 'n' Honey Cookies.

3. Cook cornmeal and coconut milk for Simple Butter. While it is cooking, blend Tofu Sour Cream, and place in containers to store in refrigerator. Blend Simple Butter and store.

4. If you have time, make 1 recipe Simple Cheese Sauce (p. 26).

DAY ONE

Fluffy Brown Rice (p. 49) (cook 2 cups = 6 cups cooked rice)

Soft Corn Tortillas (p. 43)

Cucumber Picadillo (p. 49) (or purchased salsa)

diced avocado

Cuban Black Beans (p. 49)

Tofu Sour Cream (p. 58)

1. About 45 minutes before mealtime, start cooking rice. Cook 2 cups—more than needed for one meal. Store the rest in the refrigerator to use later in the week.

2. Begin cooking Soft Corn Tortillas, one at a time, and stack between tea towels on a plate for serving. While they cook you can be dicing the vegetables in the next step.

3. Make Cucumber Picadillo and dice an avocado. Place in separate serving dishes.

4. Serve rice, beans, picadillo, avocado, and Tofu Sour Cream in separate dishes. Each person can dish up their own plate at the table. Soft tortillas can be filled with avocado, picadillo, etc., folded, and eaten with the hands. The main dish of beans and rice with toppings is eaten off the plate with a fork.

DAY TWO

Simple Cheese Sauce (p. 26) (1 recipe—leftover will be used later)

Santa Fe Burritos (p. 47)

Mexican rice (½ recipe) (variation of Curried Rice Pilaf [p. 52])

shredded lettuce and tomato salad

Avocado Guacamole (p. 47)

baked corn chips, purchased (or homemade [p. 43])

1. Approximately 1 hour before mealtime, or the night before, make Simple Cheese Sauce, then warm whole wheat tortillas in microwave slightly to make them more pliable. Mash about 2 cups of the black beans with a potato masher or in the food processor. Make Santa Fe Burritos according to recipe. Place in oven to bake 40 minutes before mealtime.

2. Cut lettuce fine and dice tomatoes. Place together in a serving bowl. Top with pitted black olives if desired.

3. Make guacamole. Serve with corn chips or put a spoonful on burrito on your plate and enjoy.

DAY THREE

Crispy Baked Tortilla Chips (p. 43)

Creamy Chipotle Pepper Dressing (p. 58)

Fiesta Salad (p. 44)

salsa (purchased or homemade)

1. One hour before (or the night before), make Crispy Baked Tortilla Chips.

2. About 45 minutes before mealtime, start making Creamy Chipotle Pepper Dressing by broiling peppers.

3. While the peppers are broiling, begin making Fiesta Salad according to directions.

4. Finish making making Creamy Chipotle Pepper Dressing, using the Tofu Sour Cream you made ahead.

5. Serve Fiesta Salad on chopped romaine according to directions. Tortilla chips and salsa can be eaten as a side dish.

DAY FOUR

Stuffed Baked Potatoes With Chipotle (p. 52)

steamed broccoli (see p. 51)

Basic Tossed Green Salad (p. 61)

Toasted Cheese Melt (p. 73) on whole wheat French bread or English muffins

1. One hour and 30 minutes before mealtime, preheat oven, prepare potatoes, and place in oven; bake 1 hour. Follow directions for Stuffed Baked Potatoes.

2. About 30 minutes before mealtime, prepare broccoli and put in saucepan. Place on stove 10 minutes before meal-time.

3. Prepare salad. Serve with chipotle dressing or other dressing of choice.

4. Dice avocado and tomato. Toss together and place in a small serving dish.

5. Spread French bread slices with Simple Cheese Sauce (p. 26) (use leftover), and top with sliced olives if desired. Place under on top rack of oven, under broiler, 5 minutes before mealtime.

DAY FIVE

Marinated Cucumber Salad (p. 60) (½ recipe)

Eggplant Chili (p. 48) with Lite and Tender Corn Bread (p. 48) or as Corn Pone (p. 48)

Avocado Guacamole (p. 47)

1. Day or evening before: make Marinated Cucumber Salad. Tip: a long English cucumber is just the right size to make ½ recipe. Pare, and then slice in your food processor with slicing blade for a quick prep.

2. One hour before mealtime, make Eggplant Chili, using leftover black beans. Follow recipe for Lite and Tender Corn Bread and make your chili into corn pone or serve corn bread on the side or on your plate with chili spooned over it.

3. Make guacamole to spoon on top of the corn bread and chili or corn pone.

4. Serve Marinated Cucumber Salad you made ahead.

WAYS TO USE LEFTOVERS

1. Make Tostadas or Soft Tacos (p. 43) with mashed black beans and Fiesta Salad filling. Top with and Creamy Chipotle Dressing or Avocado Guacamole.

2. Make Vegetarian Pizza (p. 30) on English muffins or whole wheat pita rounds using leftover Simple Cheese Sauce and toppings you like.

3. Make Macaroni and Cheese (p. 30) using leftover Simple Cheese Sauce.

SHOPPING LIST

Grains and Legumes

whole wheat flour: 1½ cups
long grain brown rice: 2 cups
cornmeal: 1 cup
black beans: 2½ cups

Nuts

dry-roasted peanuts: 2 cups
raw cashew nuts: 1⅔ cups

Canned Foods

coconut milk: 1 cup
1 can Worthington Vegetarian Burger (Low Fat) or Veggie Cutlets, ground (p. 37)
6-ounce can tomato paste
14.5-ounce can diced tomatoes in juice: 2 cans (for Picadillo and Chili)
unsweetened applesauce: ½ cup
pitted olives: 1 can

Produce

avocados: 4
tomatoes: 2
cilantro: 1 bunch
lime: 1
cucumbers: 3
yellow onions: 2
romaine lettuce: 1 head
sweet onion: 1 (or 3 green onions)
baking potatoes: 2
broccoli: 1 bunch
red cabbage: ½ head
carrots: 2
eggplant: 1 small
garlic: 1 bulb

Seasonings

vanilla
butter salt (Flavacol) (optional)
lemon juice
onion powder (fine grind—not granulated)
dried chives (may use fresh for Tofu Sour Cream)
garlic powder
cumin
California Chili
Wright's Hickory Seasoning
Vege-Sal or celery salt
parsley flakes, dried
basil
dill weed
poppy seeds
yeast flakes
dried onion flakes: ¼ cup (or 1 fresh onion)

Other

12-ounce box MoriNu tofu: 2 (may use similar amount regular tofu)
corn tortillas: 6
whole wheat tortillas: 12
whole wheat French bread or English muffins: 1 loaf or package
baking powder of choice
honey: ½ cup (or ¾ cup brown sugar)
molasses: 2 tablespoons

ITALIAN AND COUNTRY

DESSERT AND RECIPES TO MAKE AHEAD

carrot cake (see Create-a-Cake [p. 79]) with Maple Nut Glaze (p. 79)

Simple Butter (p. 56)

Simple Mayonnaise (p. 57)

Cashew Cream (p. 107)

1. Make carrot cake, and while it bakes, make Maple Nut Glaze. Remove from kettle and set aside to cool.

2. Using same kettle (no need to wash), cook cornmeal and coconut milk for Simple Butter.

3. While it cooks, blend Cashew Cream—you will need it for Simple Gravy (p. 26), Mashed Potatoes (p. 55), and Calzones (p. 67).

For Cashew Cream: Blend 2 cups cashews with 2 cups water until smooth. (Add more water if needed to make 3 cups total cashew cream.) Pour 2 cups of the mixture into a container and store in refrigerator. Make gravy according to directions on page 26, but omit the cashews and 1 cup of the water. Cook the gravy just before serving. Store extra gravy in refrigerator.

4. After Cashew Cream and gravy is blended and stored, blend Simple Butter and Simple Mayonnaise.

Now you are ready for simple meals this week. To make it even simpler, make Tofu-Walnut Balls (p. 41). They can be refrigerated for use in two meals, and any remaining ones can be frozen.

DAY ONE

Tofu-Walnut Balls (p. 41)

Mashed Potatoes (p. 55)

Italian Green Beans (p. 50)

Basic Tossed Green Salad (p. 61)

Ranch-style Dressing (p. 57)

Simple Gravy (p. 26)

bread or rolls with Simple Butter (p. 56)

1. About 1½ hours before mealtime, make Tofu-Walnut Balls and bake. While baking, prepare and cook potatoes for mashing.

2. Make Italian Green Beans (may use cut green beans of another kind if desired).

3. Make Basic Tossed Green Salad and Ranch-style Dressing.

4. Mash the potatoes, using about ½ cup of the Cashew Cream blended ahead with water as needed.

5. Cook Simple Gravy (blended ahead).

Make Coleslaw (p. 62) for Day Two—it tastes better if it has time to sit several hours before serving.

DAY TWO

Shepherd's Pie (p. 38)

Coleslaw (p. 62) (make the day before)

whole wheat or rye bread

Almond-Olive Spread (p. 72)

1. Approximately 45 minutes before serving time, preheat oven to 400°F and make Shepherd's Pie. Place leftover mashed potatoes in slightly flattened mounds on top of the filling.

2. Make Almond-Olive Spread.

DAY THREE

spaghetti and "meat" balls (use spaghetti sauce of choice and leftover Tofu-Walnut Balls)

Basic Tossed Green Salad (p. 61)

whole wheat French bread with Simple Butter (p. 56) and garlic (see p. 73)

1. About 30 minutes before serving time, start boiling water for spaghetti. Heat spaghetti sauce on stove or in microwave; add Tofu-Walnut Balls and heat together. Place sauce with balls in serving bowl and cooked spaghetti in a separate bowl for serving.

2. Make Tossed Green Salad and serve with dressing of choice.

3. Spread whole wheat french bread with Simple Butter and sprinkle with garlic salt. Place on cookie sheet on top shelf of oven and broil 5 minutes or until lightly toasted. Serve.

Calzones (Day Four) can be made a day ahead if desired and reheated before serving. They can also be frozen. Use made-ahead Cashew Cream (p. 107) in both the crust (Cobbler Crust [p. 88]) and the Spinach Filling (p. 67).

DAY FOUR

Calzones (p. 67) (or bread with Spinach Dip [p. 73] or Spinach Filling [p. 67]) (toasted under broiler)

Pasta Fagioli Soup (p. 68)

1. At least two hours before serving time, make Calzones, or make Broiled Open-face Spinach Toast (see p. 73).

2. About 30 minutes before serving time, make Pasta Fagioli Soup.

DAY FIVE

steamed artichokes, broccoli, or kale with Simple Mayonnaise (p. 57)

Oat Burgers (p. 35), with leftover Simple Gravy (p. 26)

(For a quicker "entrée," serve whole wheat toast with gravy.)

carrot and celery sticks

Almond-Olive Spread (p. 72) on bread or Rye Krisp

1. One hour before serving time, prepare the artichokes by cutting off the bottom stem and tips of leaves if they have sharp thorns. Cover with water in a medium saucepan and simmer for 1 hour. Serve with Simple Mayonnaise for dipping leaves and dressing the heart as you eat. Or prepare

another type of green vegetable of choice and have it ready to start cooking.

2   Make Oat Burgers. Place in oven 30 minutes before serving time and bake.

3. Make Almond-Olive Spread.

4. Heat leftover Simple Gravy.

WAYS TO USE LEFTOVERS

1. Make a whole recipe of Mashed Potatoes—you will use the leftover on the Shepherd's Pie. If there is still more left over, it can be made into patties on a cookie sheet. Sprinkle with paprika and bake in the oven under the broiler. Serve with gravy. Mashed potatoes are also useful to blend into soup (see Coconut Corn Chowder [p. 70]).

2. Use extra Oat Burgers for a "hamburger" meal. Or freeze them or use in making Hardy Hash (below).

Hardy Hash

Dice ½ cup onion, and sauté in 1 tablespoon water seasoned with salt for 2 minutes. Shred 1 cooked potato (or a leftover baked potato) into the pan after the onion is partially cooked, and add 1 Oat Burger, diced. Sprinkle with seasoned salt or salt and paprika. Stir now and then as it browns. Moisten with a tablespoon of soy milk and then serve with ketchup.

SHOPPING LIST

Grains

quick oats: 3½ cups

cornmeal: ½ cup

whole wheat flour: 2 cups

unbleached white flour: 1 cup

flaxseed meal: ½ cup (optional for carrot cake)

Nuts

raw cashew pieces: 2 cups

chopped walnuts: 1 cup

raw almonds: ½ cup

Canned

4-ounce can mushroom stems and pieces: 1 (optional for gravy)

15-ounce can diced tomatoes in juice: 2

coconut milk: 2 cups (1 can)

8-ounce can crushed pineapple in juice: 1

pitted black or green-ripe olives: ½ cup

low-fat pasta sauce of choice for spaghetti

lemon juice: ½ cup

cans tomato soup: 2 (optional for Shepherd's Pie)

Frozen

cut green beans: 20 ounces

chopped spinach: 10 ounces

Produce

yellow onions: 3

potatoes to mash: enough for 8 cups diced raw

garlic: 1 bulb

romaine lettuce: 1 head

purple cabbage: small amount to shred for salad

salad greens if desired: 1 package

green cabbage: ½ head

kale: 1 bunch

celery: 1 bunch

artichokes: 2 (or another green vegetable of choice)

Other

16-ounce bricks tofu: 2

activated dry yeast: 1 tablespoon

cornstarch

agar powder: ½ teaspoon

soy milk: ¼ cup

baking powder of choice for carrot cake

whole wheat bread: 1 loaf (or rye bread)

whole wheat rolls: 6

whole wheat french bread: 1 loaf

burger replacement (p. 35): 2 cups

Seasonings

butter-flavored salt (optional—may use salt)

onion powder

garlic powder

Vege-Sal

Italian seasoning

basil: ¼ cup fresh or ½ teaspoon dried

Chicken-Like Seasoning

Beef-Like Seasoning

food yeast flakes

Bragg Liquid Aminos or soy sauce

dried onion flakes: ¼ cup

Ranch-style Dressing Mix seasonings (p. 57 or purchased)

CURRY, STEW, AND PASTA

DESSERT AND RECIPES TO MAKE AHEAD

Whipped Topping (p. 99)

Lemon Cream Pie (p. 87)

Raspberry Dressing (p. 60)

Tofu Sour Cream (p. 58)

Simple Butter (p. 56)

Note: This week may be simplified by choosing not to make the Lemon Cream Pie and Whipped Topping. Or just make the pie without the topping—it's still very good. If you don't make Whipped Topping, omit the Creamy Waldorf Salad (p. 62).

1. Start Whipped Topping recipe by cooking 2 teaspoons powdered agar in 1 cup water for 1 minute.

2. Remove to blender and, using same saucepan, boil together the cornmeal and coconut milk. While it simmers for 5 minutes, blend the Whipped Topping ingredients and store in a 1-quart container in refrigerator. Then blend the butter; put in containers and refrigerate. Don't wash saucepan—you'll need it again.

3. Blend Lemon Cream Pie filling and pour into saucepan. Set on stove, but don't turn it on yet. First make the Crumble Nut Crust (p. 83) and bake. While it is baking, cook the pie filling. Pour the cooked and thickened pie filling into the baked crust. Cool uncovered in the refrigerator. After several hours or overnight, reblend the Whipped Topping and spread over the surface of the cooled Lemon Cream Pie. Ready to cut and serve. Leftover Whipped Topping may be frozen or used in Waldorf Salad.

4. Make Raspberry Dressing and Tofu Sour Cream and refrigerate. If you're running out of time, skip the Raspberry Dressing and make Ranch-style Dressing (p. 57) with the sour cream. Serve on Basic Tossed Green Salad (p. 61) instead of Citrus Walnut Tossed Salad (p. 60).

DAY ONE

Fluffy Brown Rice (p. 49)

Creamed Asparagus (p. 27) or à la King Supreme (p. 27)

Citrus Walnut Tossed Salad (p. 60)

Raspberry Dressing (p. 60)

bread and Simple Butter (p. 56)

1. At least 45 minutes before mealtime, start the brown rice. Use 2 cups rice in 4 cups water with salt. This is more rice than you will need for this meal, but it will be used later.

2. Follow Creamed Asparagus or à la King recipe. Blend cream sauce while vegetables are simmering, then combine and keep covered and warm while making the tossed salad. Raspberry Dressing should have been made already.

3. Serve bread with butter.

DAY TWO

steamed broccoli or Steamed Kale (p. 51)

toast with Egglike Salad Sandwich spread (p. 75)

Chick Stew (p. 37)

1. About 45 minutes before mealtime, prepare broccoli or kale and place in medium-sized kettle to cook. Start cooking kale 30 minutes before mealtime. For broccoli, begin cooking 5-10 minutes before mealtime.

2. Make Egglike Salad Sandwich spread and put in a serving dish.

3. Make Chick Stew, following recipe directions.

DAY THREE

baked potatoes with Simple Butter (p. 56) or chili

toast and avocado slices

Chili With Corn (p. 48)

Creamy Waldorf Salad (p. 62) (½ recipe)

1. Place potatoes in oven at 400°F 1 hour before mealtime. Baked potatoes are delicious with chili, Tofu Sour Cream, and avocado slices. Or place avocado slices on toast, cover with chili, and top with Tofu Sour Cream. Delicious!

2. Make the chili.

3. About 30 minutes before mealtime, make Creamy Waldorf Salad (if you have Whipped Topping made ahead). Otherwise, make a Basic Tossed Green Salad. Instead of serving with dressing, stir into the salad a tablespoon of Tofu Sour Cream and a teaspoon of Ranch-style Dressing Mix (p. 57).

DAY FOUR

steamed greens of choice (p. 51)

Thai-Style Curry (p. 33)

Fluffy Brown Rice (p. 49)

raw carrots and celery

whole wheat tortillas and Humus Tahini (p. 58) (optional)

1. Prepare greens and begin cooking in time for them to be finished just before mealtime.

2. Make a whole recipe of curry. It keeps for a week in a cold refrigerator and can be enjoyed again. Use rice saved from an earlier meal.

3. Prepare carrot and celery sticks. An authentic accompaniment to Indian curry would be whole wheat tortillas warmed while wrapped in a tea towel in the microwave, or wrapped in foil and heated in the oven. Serve with Humus Tahini.

Day Five

Basic Tossed Green Salad (p. 61) with dressing of choice

whole wheat French bread with Simple Butter (p. 56) if desired

Macaroni and Cheese (p. 30)

frozen edamame (green soybeans in pod—see p. 103)

frozen peas

1. About 45 minutes before mealtime, make tossed salad. Spread French bread with butter and sprinkle with garlic salt if desired. Place under broiler 5 minutes before serving.

2. Then 30 minutes before mealtime, start a kettle of salted boiling water for macaroni, and blend the cheese sauce. Boil the frozen edamame in salted water for 5 minutes.

3. Finish cooking Macaroni and Cheese according to recipe. Add frozen peas if desired (or serve peas separately), and serve.

WAYS TO USE LEFTOVERS

1. Make Pasta Primavera (p. 29) by combining leftover creamed à la King or curry with cooked pasta and heat to serving temperature. Serve with Stuffed Italian Bread (p. 66).

2. Make Creamy Rice Cereal (p. 15) for breakfast, or make Curried Rice Pilaf (p. 52) with leftover rice.

3. Use leftover steamed greens or broccoli on pizza. If you don't have pizza crust, use purchased pita or Mediterranean flat bread or English muffins. Spread with Simple Cheese Sauce (p. 26) and combine ½ cup or more chopped cooked greens with seasoned tomato sauce. Gently spoon it over the cheese sauce and add sliced olives and a sprinkling of pine nuts. Bake in hot oven until it begins to brown on the edges. Serve with soup or salad.

4. You will have leftover Whipped Topping if you make a whole recipe. Freeze it or use it for breakfast on French Crepes (p. 19).

SHOPPING LIST

Grains and Legumes

long grain brown rice: 2 cups

cornmeal: 2 tablespoons

potato flour: 2 tablespoons (optional for Mayonnaise)

Nuts and Dried

raw cashew nuts: 2½ cups

dry-roasted peanuts: ¼ cup (or 2 tablespoons peanut butter)

almonds or walnuts (for Creamy Waldorf Salad): ½ cup

Canned Foods

garbanzos (for à la King Supreme): 1 can

water chestnuts (for à la King Supreme): 1 small can

mandarin oranges: 1 small can

lemon juice or fresh lemon: ¼ cup

coconut milk: 3 cans

15-ounce can diced tomatoes in juice: 2

15-ounce can small red or black beans: 1

8-ounce can tomato sauce: 1

pickles: 1 or 2

garbonzos or black beans: 1 can (or use 2 cups lentils [for Thai-style Curry])

Frozen

peas: 3 cups

corn: 2½ cups

edamame (green soy beans in pod): 12 ounces

raspberries, unsweetened: 1 cup

apple juice concentrate: ½ cup

Produce

asparagus: 1 bunch (omit if making à la King Supreme)

yellow onions: 5

red bell pepper: 2

green bell pepper: 1

mushrooms: 2 cups sliced (or canned)

romaine lettuce: 1 head (or salad greens)

cucumber (for salad): 1

sugar snap peas (for salad): 1 cup (optional)

cilantro: 1 bunch (see p. 115, hint)

carrots: 4

celery: 4 sticks

avocado: 1 large

apples: 2 or 3 Fuji or other sweet

broccoli or kale: 1 bunch

garlic: 1 head

potatoes: 2 baking and 2 red

zucchini: 6-8 small (used in two recipes)

Other

honey or sweetener of choice: 1 cup

molasses: 2 tablespoons

cornstarch or Clear Jel: 3 tablespoons

Soy Curls: 1 cup (for Chick Stew—may use canned gluten product or diced Veggie Cutlets [p. 37])

tofu, firm: 8 ounces

MoriNu Silken Soft Tofu: 12 ounces

fettuccini (or macaroni): ½ pound (see p. 104, whole grain pasta)
whole wheat tortillas and ingredients for Humus Tahini, a suggested accompaniment to go with Thai-style Curry on Day Four.

⅓ cup soy milk powder

Holiday Menu and the Week After

DESSERT AND RECIPES TO MAKE AHEAD

Pumpkin Pie (p. 86)

Veggie Cutlets (p. 37)

Bread Dressing (p. 36)

Simple Butter (p. 56)

Simple Mayonnaise (p. 57)

1. **Make** Simple and Flaky Piecrust **(p. 83), but don't bake. Make pumpkin pie filling and bake in crust. (Good served with** Whipped Topping **(p. 99), or ice cream, and maybe by now you have some left over in the freezer. Pie is good by itself too!)**

2. **Make Veggie Cutlets and bake at the same time the pie is baking.**

3. **Make bread cubes for** Bread Dressing **(p. 36). Make the Bread Dressing if you have time, place in baking pan, and store in refrigerator.**

4. **Make Simple Butter followed by Simple Mayonnaise. (You don't have to wash out the blender after the butter.)**

DAY ONE

Bread Dressing (p. 36)

baked potatoes or Stuffed Baked Potatoes (p. 52) (optional—they can be baked in the oven at the same time as the Bread Dressing)

Veggie Cutlets (p. 37)

Simple Gravy (p. 26)

Sugar Peas and Carrots in Lime Sauce (p. 50) (½ recipe)

1. **About 1¼ hours before serving time, make Bread Dressing. If you made it ahead, put it in the oven 1 hour before serving time. (Put potatoes in oven at this time too if you decide to serve them.) Or make stove-top variation in a nonstick skillet 15 minutes before serving time.**

2. **Make broth for Veggie Cutlets and slice one loaf into thin slices. Simmer in the broth for 5 minutes.**

3. **Make Simple Gravy; keep on stove on warm temperature until ready to serve.**

4. **Make Sugar Peas and Carrots in Lime Sauce.**

5. **Place Bread Dressing in a serving platter and arrange Veggie Cutlets on top, or serve in a separate casserole dish.**

DAY TWO

oven French Fries (p. 55)

cutlet salad sandwiches in whole wheat bagels or burger buns (see p. 74)

Simple Mayonnaise (p. 57)

ketchup

1. **About 40 minutes before mealtime, preheat oven to 450°F and cut potatoes into French Fries. Place in oven 20 minutes before mealtime if precooked; 30 minutes if not precooked.**

2. **Arrange sliced tomato, lettuce, and pickles on a plate. Serve mayonnaise in a small bowl, and bagels or buns sliced and ready to use in a basket.**

3. **Serve French Fries as soon as they are baked. They are best freshly baked and hot!**

DAY THREE

brown rice or pasta

steamed broccoli

Creamy Stroganoff (p. 29) (whole recipe)

whole wheat rolls or bread

Simple Butter (p. 56)

1. **About 45 minutes before mealtime, cook rice. If pasta is used, prepare 15 minutes before mealtime.**

2. **Prepare broccoli and place in a small saucepan, ready to cook 10 minutes before mealtime.**

3. **Make Creamy Stroganoff.**

DAY FOUR

Armenian Lentil Soup (p. 69) (½ recipe, or make whole recipe and freeze extra)

Pita (Pocket) Bread (purchased or make your own) (p. 64)

Avocado Dip (p. 69) (½ recipe)

or cutlet salad sandwich filling (see p. 74)

or Humus Tahini (p. 58)

1. **About 1½ hours before mealtime, start making the soup. (It can be made earlier or the day before.)**

2. **If making homemade Pita (Pocket) Bread, do it in the morning. Or make it several days ahead and freeze.**

3. **Make sandwich filling or Humus Tahini, and serve in a bowl. Make a platter of veggies to go in Pita (Pocket) Bread—sliced or diced tomato, sliced cucumber, pitted olives, and lettuce.**

DAY FIVE

Bread Dressing Casserole (p. 115)

Creamed Potatoes and Peas (p. 55)

Carrot and Raisin Salad (p. 62)

or Basic Tossed Green Salad (p. 61)

1. **About 1 hour before mealtime, make Bread Dressing Casserole. Preheat oven and place in oven 30 minutes before serving time.**

2. **Make Creamed Potatoes and Peas.**

3. Make Basic Tossed Green Salad. Serve with dressing of choice.

WAYS TO USE LEFTOVERS
1. The Creamy Stroganoff is not an easy recipe to cut in half, so make a whole recipe. Serve it on rice one day and on fettuccini (or pasta of choice) another time. The rest is used in Bread Dressing Casserole.

2. Make cream of broccoli soup (see p. 70), with extra broccoli.

3. Make Vegetarian Pizza (p. 30) on extra Pita (Pocket) Bread rounds, or serve Crispy Baked Pita Chips (p. 43). Either will make a fine accompaniment to broccoli or lentil soup.

BREAD DRESSING CASSEROLE
2 cups leftover **Bread Dressing** (p. 36)

1½ cups leftover **Creamy Stroganoff** (p. 29) (or 1 cup **Simple Gravy** [p. 26] and ½ cup diced **Veggie Cutlets** [p. 37])

1 yellow crookneck squash, diced small (about ¾ cup)

½ cup finely chopped walnuts

Mix all together and bake at 350°F for 30 minutes, until crusty on top and bottom.

SHOPPING LIST
Grains and Legumes
long grain brown rice: 2 cups

unbleached flour: 2 tablespoons

gluten flour: 2½ cups

dry soybeans: 1 cup (or use canned garbanzos for Veggie Cutlets)

lentils: 1½ cups

Nuts and Dried
raw cashews: 2 cups

raisins: 1 cup

pitted dates: ½ cup

Canned Foods
15-ounce cans garbanzos: 2 (or dry soybeans for Veggie Cutlets)

4-ounce can mushroom stems and pieces: 1 (optional for gravy)

pickles: 3

lemon juice: 2 tablespoons

14.5-ounce can diced tomatoes in juice: 1

8-ounce can water chestnuts: 1

15-ounce can pumpkin: 1

13-ounce can coconut milk: 1

Frozen Foods
chopped spinach: 1 cup

green peas: 1 cup

Produce
celery: 3 sticks

yellow onions: 3

sweet onion: small (optional for Avocado Dip)

carrots: 10

sugar snap peas: 2 cups (or frozen)

romaine or green leaf lettuce: 1 head

slicing tomato: 1

roma tomatoes: 2

baking potatoes: 4 or 5

red potatoes: 2 medium

red bell pepper: 1

cilantro: 1 bunch (snip ends off stems and store with stems in 1 inch of water in a covered container—keeps for two weeks in refrigerator.)

avocado: 1 large

broccoli: 1 bunch

sliced mushrooms: 2 cups (for stroganoff, may use canned)

limes: 2

Other
whole wheat bread: 1 loaf

whole wheat rolls: 4 (optional)

whole wheat Pita (Pocket) Bread: 1 package

honey: ½ cup (or other sweetener for pie)

cornstarch: ¼ cup

sesame tahini: 2 tablespoons (optional for Humus)

Seasonings
coriander

ginger

onion powder

garlic powder

Italian seasoning

sage

paprika

dill weed

cumin

parsley flakes

food yeast flakes

Chicken-Like Seasoning

Beef-Like Seasoning

vanilla

maple flavoring

My mother became a Christian about a year before I was born. She believed that God took interest even in the food she ate, so she became a vegetarian. My dad had no interest in this type of diet or in becoming a Christian, so Mother went on serving Daddy his roast beef, chicken, and steaks while quietly eating her vegetables. My brother Bill sided with his dad at the dinner table, expressing his disgust over any unusual foods Mother would bring to the table.

In order not to upset them, Mother would slip my sister Linda and me some vegetarian treats in another room. One of our favorites was canned "hot dogs" made from soy. Then at the table Daddy would try to slip us a piece of bacon when Mother wasn't looking. I was small for my age and naturally skinny. I can still hear my dad saying to me at the dinner table, "Better eat your roast beef, Neva. We don't want you to dry up and blow away!" Almost every Sunday my grandmother would treat the family to a meal in a nice restaurant. This was in the 1950s, when vegetarian menu selections were zero. Mother would always order the same thing—a baked potato and dinner salad—willing to stand alone, in spite of her family's obvious embarrassment over her unusual selection. Dad and Bill always ordered a nice steak, and Linda and I usually had salmon.

As the years went by, my dad gradually mellowed, and when he was in his late 50s Daddy opened his heart to God and became a Christian. About this time I met Jim Brackett at college. I had prayed that God would send a Christian man for me to share my life with, and I knew Jim was the answer to my prayers. Soon after we were married Jim introduced me to his uncle Harry and aunt Velda. They were both medical doctors who liked to study physiology and how health is affected by what we eat.

At that time doctors generally looked at vegetarianism as a deficient diet, but Uncle Harry always had new scientific research to indicate that modern diseases are caused by food high in fat, protein, and cholesterol—primarily meat, and even dairy products. On one visit Uncle Harry gave us a simple brain physiology lesson, linking diet and brain function. This added a spiritual element to diet—wholesome food leads to clear thinking and the ability to discern right from wrong. We would come home determined to make new changes in our lifestyle.

All of this presented great challenges for me, because I was not a born cook—and I didn't enjoy entertaining. Jim was an extrovert and loved to have friends over. Having just emptied the pantry and refrigerator of fats and dairy products, I couldn't imagine what to make for company. I still have a clear memory of the aftermath of one of those visits to Uncle Harry's, kneeling down in my kitchen and praying, "Yes, Lord, I want to follow all Your instructions. I've cleaned up my kitchen; now You'll have to teach me how to cook." (I'm thankful I didn't know that God would teach me to cook by putting me in charge of cooking schools and a vegetarian restaurant!)

During this time I would tell my mother about the changes I was making, but she wasn't convinced. In the 1970s the evidence wasn't very strong in favor of a vegan diet. She started feeling annoyed whenever we would bring up Uncle Harry. Then the media began carrying reports about the benefits of a wholly plant-based diet. Mother loved cheese the most, but finally decided to try cooking without it. One by one she eliminated the other high-fat foods from her diet. Now

> *I was not a born cook and I didn't enjoy entertaining. I couldn't imagine what to make for company.*

my mother, who all her life had struggled with her weight, saw the unwanted pounds disappear. She had never before lost weight without dieting and feeling hungry and deprived all the time. But now she learned that she could eat her fill of unrefined foods, and the pounds melted away.

Daddy ate her food—and his, too. He loved to snack on slices of cheese when he came home hungry from a day's work. But Mother never nagged him about it. Then my dad came home from a visit to the family doctor with a bottle of pills and the news that

Outside seating at Five Loaves Deli and Bakery

he had high blood pressure. Mother told him he wouldn't have to take those pills if he would just eat the way she did, so he agreed. On his next visit to the doctor his blood pressure was normal—and he never had to take the pills. An amazing side benefit of eliminating dairy products was that his hay fever disappeared.

Meanwhile, God kept helping me learn to cook. Since Jim's palate had been refined by his perfectionist German mother, he was fond of rich foods. He wasn't sure if eating would ever be fun again. I had been raised opening cans and thawing frozen meals. I couldn't even cook rice. But the cook in the family,

my German mother-in-law, joined our quest to replace the old favorites with new versions that Jim would like. We became a team, sharing ideas over the phone. We both had a sense that God would want us to eat well, to live well, and to enjoy what we ate. So we prayed a lot in the kitchen, and God blessed our efforts. Eventually my mother-in-law and I published our first cookbook, *Something Better,* in 1981.

We really believed that God had given us the secret to low-fat cooking. He had provided "something better" than the old favorites we had given up. I raised my two daughters on those wholesome recipes, and today they are raising their children the same way. In 1989 we started a restaurant in Seattle—Five Loaves Deli and Bakery, where I tried out my recipes on the public. The response was enthusiastic. The customers came back for more. Trying to please customers made me refine my recipes. I worked with a fine team of cooks from varied backgrounds. Many prayers went up from the Five Loaves kitchen as we worked together to make food that would appeal to all kinds of people. As a result, after several years of operation *Best Gourmet Recipes* was published in 1995.

Best Gourmet Recipes has been updated five times—the additions and variations are the result of making recipes over and over and learning ways to improve and simplify the process. In 1999, after operating our restaurant for nearly 10 years, we closed its doors and moved to Reno, Nevada, where Jim and I serve as health educators. Part of Jim's job is to hold seminars on reversing diabetes, heart disease, and obesity. I serve meals to the participants, and teach them the secrets God has taught me. We have given seminars to Navajo Native Americans in Utah and to islanders in Barbados and St. Lucia in the Caribbean. Adaptations had to be made for some of the recipes to be useful in other cultures, but the basic principles of a healthy diet have proved true everywhere.

Best Gourmet Recipes is still selling well, and again and again people tell us, "I love your book. It's my favorite cookbook. All the recipes turn out good!" And that's why we decided to publish *Seven Secrets*.

The name of our restaurant, Five Loaves Deli and Bakery, came from the story of the little lad who shared his lunch with Jesus. After seating a crowd of 5,000 hungry people on the grassy hillside, Jesus took the child's basket of five loaves and two fishes, blessed the food, and handed it out to the multitude. It multiplied in His hands so much that after everyone had had their fill there were 12 baskets left over.

And that's what God has done for me. He took me as a novice and blessed my efforts. I was so afraid the night before my first cooking class that I couldn't sleep. In desperation I prayed, and God brought to my mind the story of the loaves and fishes in Mark 6:34-42. Then I found these encouraging words in a classic commentary on the life of Christ, *The Desire of Ages*, by E. G. White, and that story has been my source of inspiration ever since.

"The miracle of the loaves teaches a lesson of dependence upon God. . . . The means in our possession may not seem to be sufficient for the work; but if we will move forward in faith, believing in the all-suffi-cient power of God, abundant resources will open before us. If the work be of God, He Himself will provide the means for its accomplishment. He will reward honest, simple reliance upon Him. The little that is wisely and economically used in the service of the Lord of heaven will increase in the very act of imparting. In the hand of Christ the small supply of food remained undiminished until the famished multitude were satisfied. If we go to the Source of all strength, with our hands of faith outstretched to receive, we shall be sustained in our work, even under the most forbidding circumstances, and shall be enabled to give to others the bread of life" (pp. 368-371).

After reading that, I knew that God cared whether or not my food samples would be appealing and sufficient at the class the next day. In the years that followed, I often turned to that Bible story whenever I felt overwhelmed in the kitchen. And so today this new cookbook goes out with a prayer that each kitchen in which these recipes are made will become the source of new life for all who partake of its nourishment. So if you are feeling a little overwhelmed at the idea of cooking this new way, ask God to help you—and He will!

—Neva Brackett

Neva and Jim at Five Loaves, one of two vegetarian restaurants opened in Seattle

Perhaps more than anything you want your children to like healthy foods. Be patient with them and keep trying different recipes to find ones they like. Have them help you in the kitchen if they are interested—kids usually will eat what they make!

We've picked out some recipes that even picky eaters might enjoy eating or making. These recipes have been tested on our own grandchildren and many of their little friends.

You can make cupcakes, muffins, or even doughnuts with Create-a-Cake batter. I make doughnuts with my grandchildren in a Teflon doughnut pan that I bought at a specialty kitchen store. Pour the batter in the doughnut-shaped depressions and bake in the oven as you would muffins. Spread lightly with a glaze such as Maple Nut Glaze. The children love to decorate with purchased colored sprinkle shapes.

Lee Ann and Ralene making doughnuts in Grandma Neva's kitchen

TOPICAL INDEX

*Indicates wheat-free or wheat-free variation

RECIPE INDEX

RECIPE INDEX

RECIPE INDEX

Introducing the
FAMILY BIBLE STORY
series

Unlike any other Bible story books you've ever seen, this series offers something special for every member of the family. The *Family Bible Story:*

- Helps kids discover fascinating facts about the Bible
- Creates trust in the authenticity of the Bible
- Bridges the gap between the biblical and modern world

- Builds a moral foundation for day-to-day living
- Enriches your family worship experience
- Makes Bible stories come alive

Author Ruth Redding Brand carefully researched each biblical story and explored the Holy Land with world-renowned archaeologist Siegfried Horn to add an authenticity of detail that makes the Family Bible Story *series live and breathe.*

FOR MORE INFORMATION
- Visit www.TheBibleStory.com
- or write
  Home Health Education Service
  PO Box 1119
  Hagerstown, MD 21741

MORE FAMILY READING

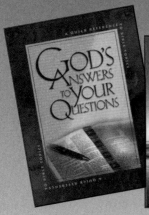

**God's Answers
to Your Questions**
You ask the
questions; it points
you to Bible texts
with the answers

**He Taught
Love**
The true meaning
hidden within the
parables of Jesus

**Jesus, Friend
of Children**
Favorite
chapters from
The Bible Story

Bible Heroes
A selection
of the most
exciting adven-
tures from
The Bible Story

The Storybook
Excerpts from
Uncle Arthur's
Bedtime Stories

My Friend Jesus
Stories for
preschoolers from
the life of Christ,
with activity page

**Quick and Easy
Cooking**
Plans for complete,
healthful meals

**Fabulous Food for
Family and
Friends**
Complete menus
perfect for
entertaining

**Choices:
Quick and
Healthy
Cooking**
Healthy meal
plans you can
make in a hurry

**More Choices
for a Healthy,
Low-Fat You**
All-natural meals
you can make in
30 minutes

**Tasty Vegan
Delights**
Exceptional
recipes without
animal fats or
dairy products

**Fun With
Kids in the Kitchen
Cookbook**
Let your kids help
with these healthy
recipes

Health Power
Choices you can make
that will revolutionize
your health

Secret Keys
Character-building
stories for
children

Winning
Gives teens
good reasons to
be drug-free

FOR MORE INFORMATION:
- or visit www.TheBibleStory.com
- or write
  Home Health Education Service
  PO Box 1119
  Hagerstown, MD 21741

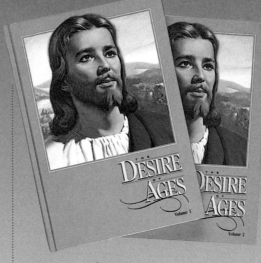

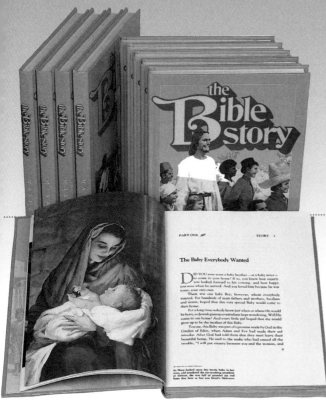
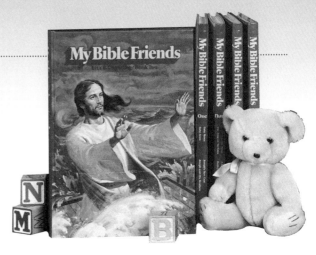
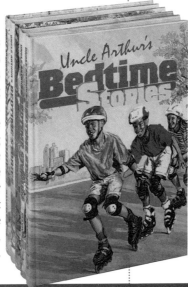

Share Good Health

Tell your friends, coworkers, family members, or neighbors that you've found valuable secrets for:

- ✔ **Losing weight**
- ✔ **Eating smarter**
- ✔ **Exercising effectively**
- ✔ **Finding peace of mind**
- ✔ **Knowing God better**

Surprise them with a gift subscription to *Vibrant Life*. They'll recognize right away that you care about their health and happiness.

Order one subscription to *Vibrant Life* for US$19.95 (one year, six issues), then send a second subscription anywhere in the U.S.A. for free. Please add US$7.00 for each address outside the U.S.A. Offer subject to change.

When you share *Vibrant Life* gift subscriptions, you're spreading good health in a friendly, loving way.

"Buy One, Share One Free"

Vibrant Life
MAGAZINE

DON'T WAIT.
Order a gift subscription today!

Send **subscriptions** to:

Your name_____

Address_____

City_____State_____Zip_____

Phone_____

Gift name_____

Address_____

City_____State_____Zip_____

Phone_____

Payment options:

❏ Payment enclosed

❏ Charge my credit card
#_____

Exp. date_____

Mail to: Subscriber Services
P.O. Box 1119, Hagerstown, MD 21741
Call 1-800-765-6955 or visit **www.vibrantlife.com**

F05-01-0